DATE DUE

Demco, Inc. 38-293

MAY 0 3 2011

BROADCAST, INTERNET, AND TV MEDIA IN THE ARAB WORLD AND SMALL NATIONS

Studies in Recent Developments

BROADCAST, INTERNET, AND TV MEDIA IN THE ARAB WORLD AND SMALL NATIONS
Studies in Recent Developments

Edited by
Jabbar Audah Al-Obaidi
and
William G. Covington, Jr.

With a Foreword by
Shakir Mustafa

The Edwin Mellen Press
Lewiston•Queenston•Lampeter

Library of Congress Cataloging-in-Publication Data

Broadcast, internet, and tv media in the Arab world and small nations : studies in recent developments / edited by Jabbar Audah Al-Obaidi, William G. Covington, Jr. ; with a foreword by Shakir Mustafa.
    p. cm.
  Includes bibliographical references and index.
  ISBN-13: 978-0-7734-1302-3
  ISBN-10: 0-7734-1302-2
  1. Mass media--Arabic countries--History--21st century. 2. Mass media--Developing countries--History--21st century. 3. Mass media--Social aspects--Arab countries x History--21st century. 4. Mass media--Social aspects--Developing countries x History--21st century. I. 'Ubaydi, Jabbar' Awdah. II. Covington, William G.
  P92.A65B76 2010
  302.230917'4927--dc22

                              2010022432

hors série.

A CIP catalog record for this book is available from the British Library.

Front cover illustration by Dave Wilson

The Edwin Mellen Press
Box 450
Lewiston, New York
USA 14092-0450

The Edwin Mellen Press
Box 67
Queenston, Ontario
CANADA L0S 1L0

The Edwin Mellen Press, Ltd.
Lampeter, Ceredigion, Wales
UNITED KINGDOM SA48 8LT

Printed in the United States of America

Dedication

For our beloved families and highly appreciated graduate and undergraduate students who made this modest effort possible.

TABLE OF CONTENTS

Foreword

To call the circumstances surrounding a political event such as the Iranian Presidential elections last month a "twitter revolution" must be a sign of the times.

Texting, emails, and twitter do keep people connected on a daily basis, but observers of the recent turmoil in Iran must have noticed how such connections continue to make a tremendous impact on the local and world political stages. Twitter is truly the Mighty Bird of a new, brave age that still seems to relish the power of symbolic phenomena. Brisk communications that go small but whose reach is limitless.

It must also be a sign of the times that a cliché depicting the world's "shrinkage" into a manageable village slaps us now time and again with renewed vigor. The globe has almost suddenly become frighteningly accessible, and that access is getting better, easier and cheaper with every passing day. No wonder, then, that globalization and its derivatives in all living languages have been on every tongue.

We, the scattered inhabitants of that swelling village, do think, behave, touch, see, dress, eat, speak, and feel in ways that bring us closer in manners unparalleled in previous decades and centuries. Older viewpoints of the world that seemed hostage to notions of rich and poor are giving way to fresher looks that centralize access to, not just availability of, resources.

This new book about global communications makes these worldwide and apparently overwhelming realities its springboard to sharp and topical investigations of pressing challenges. Not only the complex issues of communications are the subject matter here, but also the contexts in which they should be comprehended. Of central and immediate relevance in such an approach is the extended inquiry into the implications and consequences of a vast transformation of our times. For instance, the opening chapters clearly mindful of the cultural and social implications of an objective and descriptive discussion of media organizations in the interactive global environment. Its elaborate look at the value of "intuition" is testimony to the role of an elusive, personal element in contemporary scientific debates. The impact of a personal element makes another appearance in chapter six that demonstrates its argument with the life story of one individual, Vladas.

It is not my intention to talk about the chapters of this book since the book's introduction does that, but I will briefly highlight cohesive matters of particular interest in the individual contributions to this volume. Chapters two, four, and seven, for example, conveniently break down the diverse communicative scene in the Middle East, especially the Arab World, to show the intricate relations between the media and several civic institutions molding daily life in that region.

The pace of global communications has energized the winds of change there as the chapters demonstrate the rise of unofficial, courageous journalism. Similarly, chapters three and five offer an extended investigation into the interaction of new complex developments in the media with students and educators on American campuses. Now, the need to cope with complex media material and dissemination is rapidly becoming a daily classroom subject.

The diverse issues the book deals with are well complimented with the diverse backgrounds of its research team. Immediate and accurate knowledge of contexts and surrounding circumstance certainly makes a difference in academic inquiry. This is quite visible in virtually all chapters where social, political, cultural, and personal contexts and experiences come to bear upon descriptive analyses of media matters. Such knowledge of contexts and surroundings becomes indispensable in the chapters on Arab media, a field in which reliable sources in English are extremely scarce.

The book thoughtfully includes an extensive bibliography that should provide researchers with a valuable resource and a reminder that academic discourse continues to pick up and move on where others end.

Dr. Shakir Mustafa
Visiting Associate Professor
World Languages Center
Northeastern University
Boston, Massachusetts

iv

Acknowledgments

Our work on global communication and media in relations to communication technologies has expanded over the last decade. Colleges and universities have offered dozens of important courses covering topics investigating the international nature of media, discussing media convergence, and analyzing the multiple access routes to different types of media. In the context of the global growth of study, many individuals have contributed to this manuscript. We would like to thank our colleagues Muhammad I. Ayish, Joel R. Willer, Naila Hamdy, Anthony Esposito, Steven Phipps, and Bjorn Ingvoldstad, the authors of the chapters that made the bulk of this volume. Without their professionalism and expertise, this effort would not have been materialized.

Special thanks to Shakir Mustafa who dedicated part of his busy calendar to write the Foreword for this manuscript. We are grateful to our colleague James Moore who made a genuine contribution to this manuscript by ways of offering insightful suggestions and editing. We are also thankful to Dave Wilson for designing the front cover for this book. Grateful acknowledgement is made to Mrs. Patricia Schultz, Production Editor of the Edwin Mellen Press for her technical support and expertise.

Finally yet importantly, we are indebted to our current and former students who always challenge us with sophisticated questions and hence have motivated us to search for some answers to satisfy their educational needs for global connections and understanding.

Our beloved families also deserve a thank you word with heartfelt and deep appreciation for their patience, support, and unconditional love. Their consistence encouragement always helps us move forward on the road of hope and productivity.

Introduction

As a concept, global communication is hardly new to the literature of communications in general, and the practice of exchanging and transmitting information among societies in particular. People have been globally involved in communication and information exchange for centuries. (Lubbers & Koorevaar, 2000). Activities like, trade, migration, pilgrimage, exploration, and even wars have long motivated individuals and communities, to travel, to maneuver, to do business, to exchange knowledge and information, and to invent new tools for their work and communication. Therefore, one cannot underestimate the importance and the depth of transformations taking place in global communication. Thomas L. McPhail (2006) has pointed out that the "era of the Enlightenment (ca.1600-1800) contributed to the intellectual transformation of Western societies," fueled then by major new technological advancements in communications and media.

What is new today, however, consists of the expansive applications of global communication, the broad utilization of electronic media, the speed of information processes, and the ripple effects that have developed after the third phase of the communication revolution. The world has really shrunk and become a tiny global virtual village. Geographical limitations, linguistic barriers, and the level of virtual interaction with individuals living far across the world, all have drastically changed. Or as Thomas L. Friedman has described "the world is flat" (2005). Nandan Nilekani, CEO of Infosys Technologies Limited in India has addressed the revolution of communication technology and the explosion of computer use and software this way, "[all of these advancements happened and] they created a platform where intellectual work, intellectual capital, could be delivered from anywhere." (Friedman, 2005). In this way, the understanding of media convergence as "all come together" and global communication as a "free flow of information" seem to meet.

Arguably these results are thanks to a goldsmith and his contribution to the world of communications around 1439. That goldsmith was Johann Gutenberg, and he developed the mechanical process of printing via movable type. This important process made it possible to publish many copies of a single work at one time. The invention of the moveable type greatly accelerated and enabled the dissemination of cultural and cognitive changes that already had been in effect since the invention and implementation of alphabets. Today, we have satellite-connected mobile phones and laptop computers which can access search engines such as Google, Yahoo, Bing, Powerset, AltaVista, Excite and more to come.

Through the internet individuals can communicate with each other around the world via email, twitter, Facebook, MySpace, and the rest. Global media have adapted to these new developments and have started utilizing these new digital tools to reach out to their local and internal audiences. Schools, colleges, and universities are not behind either. They have adopted different levels of communication technologies to disseminate their educational content to a wider learning community. Online classes and undergraduate and graduate programs have become readily available for people around the world. The boundless nature of Internet and media technology have profoundly affected and changed the nature and work of conventional media and communication. Indeed, in the twenty-first century age of the Internet, new electronic frontiers are the highlight of global communication and media.

Meanwhile, these developments and discoveries have made governments as well as media scholars, technology experts, and professional users to lead waves of discussion concerning legal frameworks, government regulation, ownership policies, ideology, ethics, and media economics. The potential dangers of having an open path for information to travel almost freely from one point to another have been a sticking issue during the late twentieth/early twenty-first century as well. However, these concerns have not stopped the technological developments in communication. The connection between information, data, and communication technologies has become a new reality and an unavoidable phenomenon. Satellites, cables, computers, the internet, digital media, and information database technology has given birth to what we call an information society. International stories, crises, financial news, sports, music, film, and entertainment, as well as all kind of databases have become readily available to most people around the globe.

As new terms sprang to the communication surface such as *multimedia*, and *convergence*, old frontiers began to collapse in favor of faster information and communication technologies. Indeed, the late 1980s witnessed drastic changes that induced dramatic political developments in European, Asian, African, and Middle East countries. These changes brought new political structures, democratic trends, new international agreements, and most importantly introduced new communication systems. Hence, the combination of both vast information and fast paced technology generated a new understanding about global communication, an understanding that recognizes the level of technological sophistication, and that prizes the ability to transmit and receive information on a world-wide scale. However, barriers involving language, technical capability, time zone, and local coverage still stand.

This book discusses topics based on the idea of how digital media, social media, and new ways of communication have become vital to the way people live in a global-virtual village as the lives of individuals from myriad cultures and backgrounds are brought closer together in a virtual collapse of time and space. From a systems perspective, a change in one component of a subsystem has ramifications extending far beyond where the change occurred in distance and time. Indeed, the decisions that are made at an individual level reach into the lives of millions, whether they are negative or positive alterations. Each contributor in this volume examines the significance these changes are making to individuals and societies. Whether the change is in content in a local television newscast due to increased competition from media platforms, whether the change is the international influence one country exerts on another through political decisions, or whether the change is in the teaching of a single class, the principle applies. The systemic transformation is a reality. It has manifest implications and ripple effects on individuals and societies.

The focus of chapter one is on the challenges that face media management and organization in the age of an interactive global media environment. Whether one calls the environment a place of "Intellectual Capital", "Intellectual Industry", or "Virtual Colonialism," the era of globalization has re-emerged and brought with it both skepticism and optimism.

Such a global technological environment has created a set of conditions favorable to the use of multimedia to accomplish multitasks instantly. Hence, chapter two discusses new frontiers and the challenges of new technology with regard to policymaking and regulations of media in the Middle East, particularly in terms of the transformations of 'knowledge societies' and civic empowerment.

With a focus on American campus communities, chapter three addresses how in the case of higher education student media products have transformed in response to the convergence of media and the emergence of new media delivery systems. The chapter highlights some of the compelling issues facing educational systems in this time of convergence in the marketplace of the twenty-first century.

Along this line, chapter four sheds light on how technology creates a challenge to mainstream and traditional media. As well this chapter examines challenges to local authorities in relationship to regulation, law, and media policies that do not seem too appropriate for newly emerging media in general and social media in particular.

Acquiring writing skills, developing abilities to design messages for new media, and preparing students and journalists for global media of the twenty-first century are the topics for chapter five. It covers specific issues educators face in the convergence marketplace. Even though media technology continues to play a vital role in how modern day media people perform, their responsibilities as well as their professional news writing and reporting skills remain of significant importance to media managers and media faculty in colleges and universities.

Television and small-nation globalization is the topic for chapter six. It articulates the interplay between Lithuanian television and its viewers in response to technological changes in the delivery system in the country. The Lithuanian national broadcast networks continue to be popular, and both public and private channels continue to struggle to secure their viability in a globally volatile market.

In a vital geopolitical region like the Middle East, electronic media also play a significant role in the growth of a new generation. Chapter seven examines how that generation is eager to challenge its governments, regulations, and conservative social reality, in favor of using the Internet and social media. Consequently, homes, schools, colleges, and universities already have incorporated new communication technologies for daily use. In addition, chapter seven discusses the challenges and difficulties facing traditional media and traditional government, as well as traditional society.

Finally, through the various sections in this collection, scholars from different backgrounds discuss how changes in media content and delivery systems influence culture, education, international relationships, flow of information, laws and policies, and human expectations. Tracing the trends of convergence and increased competition for a fickle fragmented audience, media owners find themselves in a challenging set of circumstances. The conclusion of this book is that with the conditions and harsh global circumstances there also exists the opportunity for unprecedented success in bridging the digital gaps between rich and poor countries, and between local and international communities. Rather than being predictive, this book is largely descriptive. Some contributors devote most of their attention to a single kind of global media outlet while others view international media industries, organizations, and regulations. Such a diversity of frameworks expands the discussion. This work adds to the ongoing process of studying an ever-emerging global media industry that touches everyone on the globe and opens new frontiers for the world.

Jabbar Audah Al-Obaidi &
William G. Covington, Jr.

References and Notes

Friedman, L. Thomas (2005) *The World is Flat: A Brief History of the Twenty-First Century.* New York: Farrar, Straus &Giroux.

Grei, J. Michael (2000). Globalisation. In Jureidini & Poole "Sociology: Australian Connections (2nd Ed)" Sydney:Allen & Unwin.

Lubbers, Ruud& Koorevaar, Jolanda. (2000) *"Primary Globalisation, Secondary Globalisation, and the Sustainable Development Paradigm - Opposing Forces in the 21st Century"* in *The Creative Society of the 21st Century: Future Studies,*France:OECDpp.7-24.Alsoin:http://wiki.media-culture.org.au/index.php/Global_Communication

McPhail, L. Thomas(2006). *Global Communication: Theories, Stakeholders, and Trends.*(2nd ed).Malden, MA. Blackwell Publishing.

Chapter One

Management's Challenge of Positioning Media Organizations for the Interactive Global Media Environment

William G. Covington, Jr.
Edinboro University of Pennsylvania

Management is responsible for an organization's growth and survival through the appropriate use of resources. In the case of an ever-changing environment where the industry itself continues to adapt to new regional and global realities, the art of predicting the future and utilizing one's resources accordingly is particularly challenging.

Talcott Parsons placed social action in a theoretical framework that he saw as developing from three different schools or traditions (Devereux). Parsons viewed *utilitarians* as classical economists who had been attempting to develop essentially a rationalistic theory of individual social behavior. He saw *positivists* as attempting to develop a theory which could handle behavior in terms of determinate scientific laws such as are found in physics or biology. And finally, he considered *idealists* to be those who were seeking to come up with a theory which interpreted concrete social phenomena as essential emanations from the arena of cultural values (Devereux).

Viewing the challenges media managers faced from Parsons' framework, we might come up with a picture of *utilitarians* as being stoic in nature, expecting an evitable change in technology, audience expectations, and industry standards. *Positivists* might be considered those in the field who contend that change will happen as a force of nature, that it is unavoidable and beyond the ability of anyone to control it. While *idealists* might be viewed as media mangers who look to the audience, i.e., the marketplace to see what will emanate both in terms of content and delivery systems.

Four Systems of Action

Parsons further divided his paradigm into four systems of action which have potential for observing the changing environment in which media managers find themselves (Wallace and Wolf). It is worth noting that as a systems theorist, Parsons analyzed the individual, the broader system, various subsystems, and the role of relationships in each of these four. Depending on the approach, different components receive different emphasis.

The Cultural System

In the first system the basic unit of analysis is the "meaning" or "symbolic system." When a system of which an individual is a part shares the cultural meaning of an intangible such as discipline, value for that trait causes people to interact with each other in a certain way. The implication for media managers is twofold. On the content level it has to do with what values are being expressed implicitly or directly through programming. Within the organization, it has to do with the values that are rewarded in the workplace. Is promotion based on what is vocalized?

The Social System

Relationships in a social context is the emphasis in the social system approach. Parsons considers *plurality* and *actors* and goes on to explain that such a social system could be anything from two people interacting in a restaurant to several nations transacting business globally. For media managers it would include a job performance appraisal interview or an audience created by a newly emerging niche offered by an experimental delivery platform in cyberspace.

The Personality System

The basic unit of analysis in the personality system is the individual actor. In media management this includes the manager, department supervisors, other station personnel, and audience members. Implications for accurately using this approach as an analytical tool start with what assumptions are made about individuals. Are they seen as "motivated toward gratification"? "profit maximizers"? "self interest seeker or altruistic."

The Behavioral Organism

In the last of the four systems, Parsons considers the biological portion of an individual to be the unit of analysis. He specifically looks at the central nervous system and motor activity. This approach is shallow as it fails to consider the spiritual or mental dimensions. For the sake of making it applicable to media managers, however, one might consider that in the marketplace of audience appeals, we respond behaviorally to certain stimuli. Within the station, people can be motivated by such appeals as well.

Building on Strengths

Conventional wisdom is that an individual and an organization can improve productivity by improving areas of weakness. Organizational consultant Marcus Buckingham says this focus is misdirected, that strengths should be addressed. He says efforts are best utilized when they concentrated on the natural giftings of individuals within social units.

Buckingham (2007) uses the acronym SIGN to make his point easy to remember. (S) stands for Success, (I) stands for Instinct, (G) is Growth, and (N) means Needs. In a self-reflective manner, he says the process begins by identifying what one excels in. This identification can be confirmed by feedback.

Instinct enters into the process as the gut-reaction is manifested. He relates the growth component to one's physiology, writing:

> By now you know that the biological underpinnings of your strengths are the presence of thick branches of synaptic connections. You also know that because of nature's habit of piggybacking on existing infrastructure, you will grow the most new synaptic connections in those areas where you already have the existing ones. Here you will learn the most, come up with the most new ideas, and have the best insights.

The need component indicates that although one may be drained physically after making one's contribution, one will gain psychologically a feeling of satisfaction. An authenticity sets in, validating that a significant contribution has been made.

For media managers in the changing environment of twenty-first century, this has direct applicability. Some are gifted in technical expertise, others in personnel matters, while still others in programming. Granted, managers have to bring all the subsystems together into a single entity, but there are areas where each feels most proficient. Identifying that area and emphasizing that arena increases one's ability to contribute Buckingham argues. As a team, various members tap into the expertise of other's strengths. This is a more cooperative paradigm for management that traditional top-down approaches.

Dubrin (2001) cites the work of Jeffrey Keller in identifying the two types of people a media manager will face in seeking cooperation. A *nurturing person* is supportive of other people and promotes growth by typically looking at the good qualities in everyone. This type is contrasted with a *toxic person* who dwells on the negative, highlighting what is wrong with people, places, situations, and relationships.

Consciousness Research

Scientists researching how the brain processes information before coming to a decision offer insight that could be utilized by media managers as they work with people within the organization, in addition to seeking to reach potential audiences. Traditionally the perception was that a conscious and subconscious part of the brain received messages. However, research indicates there are varying layers of consciousness, layers that process intake in different ways.

Olson Zaltman invented the Zaltman Metaphor Elicitation Technique which seeks to probe this mysterious process. The technique is used for eliciting interconnected constructs that influence thought and behavior (Szegedy-Maszak). Marketers can directly benefit by knowing how deep metaphors drive purchasing decisions. The odd thing is that people do not realize why they are making the decisions they are making according to Zaltman. He argues that language is limiting, but images capture fragments of rich and contradictory areas of unconscious feelings.

Following up on earlier Pepsi-Coke taste tests, researchers found that Pepsi was preferred on taste. However, when company logos were shown, three out of four respondents preferred Coke. Brain scans indicated that the participants exhibited wild brain activity in the portion of the brain associated with memories and self-image when the Coke logo was visible (Szegedy-Maszak).

Enhancing Individual Creativity for the Good of Media Organization

Organizational consultant William C. Miller (1986) came up with an acronym that is useful for connecting individual creativity to the broader organizational unit. He calls it "appear" even though it actually is spelled APPEARE, with an extra E.

A=Be Aware of your current and complete situation

P=Be Persistent in your vision

P=Perceive all your alternatives

E=Entertain your Intuitive Guidance

A=Assess and select among your Alternatives

R=Be Realistic in your Actions

E-Evaluate your Results

The process Miller describes will not always follow the same sequence he explains. In tapping and utilizing the mysterious power of intuition, he says you may know what to do without any conscious consideration of other alternatives. Intuition cannot be activated at will. Intuition kicks in at surprising moments.

Passion feeds the process because of the higher sense of purpose for which one seeks to accomplish a goal. In the APPEARE process, the goal of making a positive difference is the sustaining power that fuels energy when challenges and fatigue mount. Miller fleshes out the mysterious creativity process further by describing it as "a skill, an art, and a lifestyle."

Communication Technologies and Legal and Ethical Challenges

Managers and content providers face challenges created by new delivery systems that their predecessors did not face. In seeking to enhance audience interaction, many stations added blogs—short for "web logs" on their WebPages. While most are text-based, the trend is for photo, video and audio posts to include.

Ethical and legal issues became even more serious because blogs are arranged differently on different sites. Some radio stations have a separate blog for each air personality. Some are categorized by music, movies, politics, or other interest divisions. A station's reach extends worldwide with a web presence and former residents of an area can stay in touch with the community. The interactivity of the blog engages audience members with the programming source.

A challenge arises due to the anonymity of blog contributors. Libelous comments were posted on the blog of a Bellingham, Washington's talk forum station. What complicated the matter was that the poster signed the blog using someone else's name. Program Director Debbie Chavez of KGMI-AM said, "It became clear that when you allow people to be anonymous, it brings out the worst in some of them" (Vernon). The potential for bad PR and legal liability led the station to quickly change its policy. Posters are now required to email the station with comments they'd liked posted on the blog and the station determines which ones are acceptable.

Sundar, et al. divided *interactivity* into two camps: *functional interactivity* and *contingency interactivity* (Kelleher, 2007, p. 10). Functional interactivity is described as focusing on the features of media such as response forms, discussion forums, RSS (Really Simple Syndication) and e-mail. Sometimes designers neglect to consider how people actually will use the proposed interactive feature. Contingency interactivity is identified as a process involving users, media and messages in such as way that the sender may later become the receiver and vice versa (Kelleher, 2007, p. 11). Contingency interactivity is more realistic in scope.

Necessary Skills in a Global Environment

Jannie Kirby pinpoints six skills essential for potential employees in organizations in the emerging media mix:

-The ability to gather, process, and communicate information on the Internet.

-An ability to identify appropriate technologies to accomplish specific communication needs through various delivery systems.

-Ability to edit content for websites.

-Ability to apply sophisticated technical strategies for writing, editing, and producing basic websites.

-An understating of how visual aesthetics and language work together— how image-based communication differs from and interrelates with text based communication.

-An understanding of the technical and practical necessities (planning, budgeting, scripting) of a project from idea to completion.

These skills take place in a dimension that is separate from the physical world. In cyberspace, a nonstop 24-hour-7-days-a-week means content is accessible globally by anyone with a computer. Jeffrey Brody noted, "In all of history, no merchant or corporation has ever been able to do that," going on to describe that the global nature of the Internet allows virtually unlimited global commerce to occur simultaneously as users alternate between being consumers and producers (Brody). Joshua Meyrowitz (1985) traced the early history of how location and communication were altered with the implementation of new technologies:

Communication and travel were once synonymous. Our country's communication channels were once roads, waterways, and railroads. Communication speed was limited to the speed of human travel. Even the legendary Pony Express took ten and a half days to communicate a message from Missouri to California. The invention of the telegraph caused the first break between information movement and physical movement. For the first time, complex messages could move more quickly than a messenger could carry them. With the invention and use of the telegraph, the informational differences between different places began to erode.

One fact that should not be ignored is that traditional delivery platforms still have a prominent place in the emerging media mix. Hearst-Argyle partnered with Frank N. Magid Associates to ascertain the effectiveness of television as a video-advertising medium (Malone, 2008). According to the results of 2,700 local news viewers, television was considered the primary source of news information. TV came in at 55%, the Web at 26%, and print newspapers at 14% (Malone, 2008).

Consequently, knowing how to effectively turn out messages for a decades-old medium remains essential to those entering the field.

Production Never Ends in the New Media World

With twenty-four hours access to news and information, consumer demand has created a never-ending cycle in which a news product is never put to bed as it was in the days of traditional journalism. This shift was verified by a study conducted by the Project for Excellence in Journalism and reported in its fifth annual report on the state of the business of journalism. The industry trade publication, *Broadcasting and Cable* editorialized that the challenge to broadcasters is that media companies are in a quandary on how to monetize this new model ("Risk & Reward, 2008, p. 34).

Audiences go to Internet sites for updated information in large numbers, but advertisers haven't followed (Eggerton, 2008, p. 30). Brand image of well-known media companies is still a factor when it comes to credibility. Among the findings of the Project for Excellence in Journalism (PEJ) study, three key issues emerge:

One. News consumption is continual, not an end result of a search. Advertisers have not adjusted to this new consumer behavior.

Two. News websites are not final destinations, but parts of the flow consumers have to myriad other sites.

Three. Newsrooms are to be viewed as innovative, experimental parts of the news industry, a paradigm shift from putting a product to bed in finished form (Eggerton, p. 30).

Conclusion and Summary

Parson's three traditions for social action are found among media managers in the twenty-first century. Utilitarians expect an inevitable change in technology and audiences. Positivists view these changes as a force of nature beyond anyone's control. Idealists look to the marketplace as a determinant of change.

The cultural system focuses on the symbolic meaning found within content, while the social system considers the actions of participants. The personality system views individual contributors, as the behavioral organism examines actions. Buckingham's SIGN acronym fits into the mix: S=Success I=Instinct G=Growth N=Needs.

Being aware of the influence of intuition in the decision-making process is sometimes a neglected reality. The Zaltman Metaphor Elicitation Technique elicited interconnected constructs between thought and behavior that showed that people did not realize why they were making certain choices. Audience interactions such as blogs add a dimension of content that previous media managers did not face. Functional interactivity focuses on media features, while contingency interactivity looks at the process.

In the current media environment, the process of development never ends. A product is never put to bed. Brand image is still a significant factor; however, with increased venues for checking data, accuracy and timeliness are content features that are under more scrutiny than ever.

References and Notes

Brody, Jeffrey H. 2000. "The Structure of the Internet Industry," in ed. A. N. Greco. The Media and Entertainment Industries. Boston: Allyn and Bacon

Buckingham, Marcus. 2007. Go: Put Your Strengths to Work. New York: Free Press.

Devereux, Edward C. Jr. "Parsons' Sociological Theory," In Max Black ed. The Social Theories of Talcott Parsons. Englewood Cliffs, NJ: Prentice-Hall, 1961.

Dubrin, Andrew J. 2001. (1978). Human Relations: Interpersonal, Job-Oriented Skills 7th ed. Upper Saddle River, NJ: Prentice Hall.

Eggerton, John. "Are News Habits Really Changing?" Broadcasting & Cable. March 17, 2008. p.30.

Jenkins, Henry(2001), Digital Renaissance. Technology review http://web.mit.edu/cms/People/henry3/converge.pdf

Kelleher, Tom. 2007. Public Relations Online: Lasting Concepts for Challenging Media. Thousand Oaks, CA: Sage.

Kirby, Jannie. "All About a Career in New Media," assortment,
      http://www.essortment.com/career/allcareernewsm_snhu.htm Date accessed March 1,
      2008.

Malone, Michael "Study: Local TV Easily People's Main Source for New." Broadcasting and
      Cable. http://www.broadcastingcable.com/index.asp?layout=articleID=CA6536596 Date
      posted February 28, 2008. Date accessed March 1, 2008.

Meyrowitz, Joshua. 1985. No Sense of Place. New York: Oxford University Press.

Miller, William C. 1986. The Creative Edge: Fostering Innovation Where You Work. Reading,
      MA: Addison-Wesley. "Risk & Reward," Broadcasting & Cable. March 17, 2008. p. 34.

Szegedy-Maszak, Marianne. "Mysteries of the Mind: Your Unconscious is Making Your
      Everyday Decisions," US News & World Report pp. 52-58. Feb. 28, 2005.

Vernon, Tom. "With Radio Blogs, Stations Practice the Art of the Possible," Radio World pp. 1, 6,
      8. Feb. 1, 2008.

Wallace, Ruth A. & Alison Wolf. 1986. (1980). Contemporary Sociological Theory: Continuing
      the Classical Tradition 2nd ed. Englewood Cliffs, NJ: Prentice-Hall.

Chapter Two

New Frontiers in Arab World Communications Media Contributions to Life-long Civic Culture in the 21st Century

Muhammad I. Ayish
University of Sharjah

'Knowledge society,' as a theoretical concept and a strategic vision, has captured extensive public attention around the world in the context of sweeping information, communications and socio-political transitions that draw on knowledge as a prime staple of sustainable development. Though the concept was originally coined in the late 1960s and early 1970s within the notions of 'learning societies' and 'lifelong education for all' (Mansell & Wehn, 1998), it was only in the late 1980s that it came to command remarkable popularity in the context of a global post-Cold War digital and political revolution. A UNESCO report on 'knowledge societies' notes that control of knowledge has always gone hand in hand with serious inequality, exclusion, and social conflict (UNESCO, 2005). This suggests, among other things, that newer 'knowledge societies' do not lend themselves to mere accumulation of knowledge and information infrastructures, but rather to harnessing that knowledge to promote egalitarian and liberating goals with redeeming human values. While the idea of 'information societies' derives primarily from technological breakthroughs, the concept of 'knowledge societies' embraces much broader social, ethical and political dimensions whose sustainability seems contingent on a variety of conditions, and one of them is a reliable lifelong learning system.

In 'knowledge societies,' learning is no longer envisioned as an exclusive outcome of conventional formal education settings, but has come to draw on an open life-long system in which access to knowledge defines social, political, and economic power relations in society. Lifelong learning, as a prime empowerment feature of 'knowledge societies,' is achieved through a range of tools, the most outstanding of which are media with their power to carry instant messages to huge numbers of persons across vast geographical areas. Research has shown that mass-mediated lifelong learning is central for the development of 'knowledge societies' that owe their development to a well-informed and enlightened citizenry. A UNESCO document notes that new communications technologies have had a positive impact on democratic participation, promoting in particular participation directed towards the defense of great causes or centered on civic engagement. It is through lifetime media building of civic consciousness among community members that 'knowledge societies' are able to come closer to achieving their sustainable development goals (UNESCO, 2005).

The symbiosis between media as lifelong learning vehicles and civic education as a staple for the moral, social and cultural foundations of envisioned 'knowledge societies' in the Arab World is the central theme of this chapter. Researchers have established that new Arab media, especially those associated with satellite television and the World Wide Web, perform functions that go beyond mere delivery of impartial information to audiences: they also take proactive roles in stimulating further community engagement in political processes and in constructing sound and sustainable civic consciousness among their publics. Around the world, the rise of civic journalism since the late 1980s has marked a clear departure from mainstream professional media conventions that prescribe a detached and objective role for journalists in their communities. In the Arab World, however, this advocacy media role has been rather less visible in the region's public life. A convergence of social, political, economic, and professional factors seemed to have militated against the institution of civic journalism as an enduring feature of the Arab communications landscape. State authoritarianism, global power pragmatism, Western-style journalism, and cultural underdevelopment have traditionally precluded the emergence of alternative solid media orientations with explicit civic functions. However, since the mid 1990s, the evolving Arab public sphere has given the rise to new media outlets with more proactive journalistic orientations when it comes to civic education. This chapter elaborates on the Qatar-based Al Jazeera Network as an example of an emerging Arab media institution with clear civic features that are likely to have long-term effects on the realization of a democratic Arab public sphere. Given the fact that civic education is a long-term process spanning full generations, it is clear that more independent media players of the caliber of Al Jazeera, along with newly-reformed educational systems, are bound to leave enduring civic effects on the region's populations for decades to come. However, a note of caution, media alone cannot bring about the democratic transitions needed for sustaining the type of civic culture needed for the development of 'knowledge societies.' Only through the institution of solid democratic reforms in Arabian societies would media be empowered to perform their civic education functions in the twenty-first century.

Lifelong Learning, Civic Journalism, and Knowledge Society
A Conceptual Framework

Mass media have been highly regarded around the world as central contributors to our lifelong learning experience, carrying out their educational functions in both formal and non-formal contexts (Bird, et. al., 2008). In the past two decades, this media function has been accentuated by accelerating developments in information and communications technologies (ICTs), inducing new shifts in classical teacher-centered paradigms towards more symmetrical life-long learning schemes that offer disenfranchised individuals new opportunities to contribute to their emerging 'knowledge societies.' McIntosh (2005) observes that with the continuing explosion of knowledge and the breaking down of the old fixed patterns of employment, learners are increasingly demanding a type of education that allows them to update their knowledge whenever necessary and to go on doing so throughout their working lives.

Though media engagement in lifelong learning embraces a range of knowledge subjects and skills in areas like basic literacy, health, and environment, civic education has received the broadest attention. The convergence of media, lifelong learning, and civic consciousness as pillars of 'knowledge societies', has been well-recognized in interdisciplinary scholarly works in education, communication and politics. Fretwell and Colombano (2000) note that developing knowledge of the key elements of a civil society cannot be relegated only to the initial school system, particularly in countries which are going through rapid political changes. Fostering long-term stability through education requires contributions from other institutions, including media. By keeping their audiences abreast of developments at national and international levels, media contribute to building a civic culture that motivates citizens to constructively engage in their communities' living experiences, and by doing that, media facilitate our transitions into more egalitarian 'knowledge societies' (Istance, 2008).

Lifelong Learning

Lifelong learning is defined as 'the development of human potential through a continuously-supportive process, which stimulates and empowers individuals to acquire all the knowledge, values, skills and understanding they will require throughout their lifetimes and to supply them with confidence, creativity and enjoyment in all roles, circumstances and environments' (Longworth, 2002). Cecchini (2003) notes that the European Commission's definition of lifelong learning includes 'all learning activities undertaken throughout life with the aim of improving knowledge, skills and competences within a personal, civic, and social and/or employment related perspective.' For the Council of Europe, education for democratic citizenship is understood in a lifelong learning perspective and should be seen as 'embracing any formal, non-formal or informal educational activity, including that of the family, and enabling an individual to act throughout his or her life as an active and responsible citizen respectful of the rights of others.' Fales (1996) remarks that the success of lifelong learning depends on the development of solid initial education systems that ensures smoother transitions into more advanced forms of knowledge acquisition.

The concept of lifelong learning has been promoted by a wide range of national and international organizations like UNESCO and the World Bank as an alternative form of education to offset deficiencies in institutionalized learning systems (UNESCO, 2005 and World Bank, 2003). In *'Learning: The Treasure Within'* Report (2004), a UNESCO Commission notes that 'the far-reaching changes in the traditional patterns of life require of us a better understanding of other people and the world at large; they demand mutual understanding, peaceful interchange and, indeed, harmony - the very things that are most lacking in our world today.' One of the four pillars of education highlighted in the Report emphasizes 'learning to live together, by developing an understanding of others and their history, traditions and spiritual values. A World Bank report on learning to teach in the 'knowledge society' notes that 'our societies are engaged in a complicated, and unplanned, process of transformation that is affecting the way we work, relate, live and learn (Moreno, 2005). Fretwel and Colombano (2000) note that the objective of lifelong learning, taken in the broadest sense, is to help individuals obtain the skills and knowledge to assist them in adapting to different stages of their life.

Civic Education

It has been noted that 'citizens are made, not born,' and education in formal, un-formal, or informal settings has been recognized as a leading tool for making this possible. Daniel (2006) notes that an important impact of lifelong learning may be its effect in encouraging people to become more active in their communities and in promoting a more equitable and inclusive society. In the United States, the 'We the People' initiative is one of the model learning resources in which major knowledge and attitudes are carefully brought to bear on the political system and the citizenry. UNESCO has established numerous civic education chairs around the world to promote the culture of peace, human rights, and democratic governance. According to Cogan (1998), key components of civic education include five attributes: a sense of identity; enjoyment of certain rights; fulfillment of corresponding obligations; a degree of interest and involvement in public affairs; and an acceptance of basic societal values. As a social being, human beings encounter decision-making in various social situations that demand problem-solving skills. Cogan also notes that the contents of civic education are not merely limited to the dissemination of civic knowledge to produce law-abiding persons, but are also integral components of textbooks and generic learning resources to enable every individual to acquire mature citizenship qualities.

The role of media in promoting civic culture as a fundamental pillar of democratic society, has defined media-effects research traditions in the past two decades. Studies addressing media and politics in Western societies have been cognizant of communications as major forces impacting "the fundamental ideas that people have about what the world of politics is really like' (Ranney 1983). Flannigan & Zingale (1994) note that the current media mix represents an extraordinary capacity to inform the public rapidly and in considerable depth about major political news. Since few individuals regularly experience government or politics first-hand, this capacity to inform also is the power to shape and define the political reality individuals come to know. This mediated political reality heavily influences what individuals both believe they ought to know, think, and discuss about public affairs and how they are to act and participate in public life (Bowers, 1993). However, the manner in which mainstream media carry out this civic function increasingly raises concerns.

Yankelovich (1991) points out that the news reported on by the media 'is a highly refracted version of reality as the press magnifies certain aspects of politics and down plays others, which are often more central to the issue of governing.

This objectivity-inspired journalistic orientation has given rise to disenchantment with what is traditionally described as 'watchdog' or 'fourth estate' journalism, spawning what came to be known as civic or advocacy journalism. In its basic configuration, civic journalism draws on the philosophy that journalism has an obligation to public life. It is centered on the idea that a journalist can play a role beyond reporting facts by contributing to empowering publics to become responsible citizens. Bowers et. al. (1998) note that whenever the media report on public and political matters, they engage in a civic function important to the maintenance of a democratic and representative political system. The civic journalism movement, according to some researchers, does not see journalists and their audiences as passive spectators in political and social processes, but rather as active participants. The Pew Center for Civic Journalism bases this evolving tradition on the belief that journalism has an obligation to public life and that journalism can help empower a community or it can help disable it (PEW Center, 2008). Schaffer (2004) argues that civic journalism guides media professionals on how they practice their craft; how they try to connect with their communities; and how they try to empower their readers and viewers. As access to online publishing platforms becomes more available, ordinary citizens are starting to participate in gathering and delivering news.

The genesis of civic journalism was in the 1980s, in newspapers in Columbus, Georgia and Wichita, Kansas. Since then, the movement has grown and spread throughout the U.S. newspaper world (Friedland, 2002). According to a study commissioned by the Pew Center for Civic Journalism, it was found that some form of civic journalism was practiced in at least a fifth of all American newspapers, in almost every state and in every region and there is a clear pattern of development in civic journalism content, as journalists learned in what appear to be phases (Cite). Based on a survey of the electorate to measure public awareness of and involvement in "We the People', Denton and Thorson (1994) found quite encouraging results showing that the initiative encouraged respondents to vote; gave them useful tools to assess the deluge of campaign information; and made them feel more positive toward participating news organizations.

Mass Mediated Civic Lifelong Learning in Knowledge Societies

It is clear from the above analysis that 'knowledge societies' could not be envisioned without a life-long civic educational component contributed by conventional and new media. According to a UNESCO Report (2005) on 'knowledge societies', 'information age' 'knowledge societies' differ from older 'knowledge societies' in the latter's focus on human rights and their inclusive participatory character. The report conceives the importance of basic rights as translating into the particular emphasis on: freedom of opinion and expression as well as freedom of information, media pluralism and academic freedom; the right to education and its corollary, free basic education and progress towards free access to other levels of education; and, the right to 'freely participate in the cultural life of the community, to enjoy the arts and to share in scientific advancement and its benefits'. These are the civic foundations that give rise and sustainability to 'knowledge societies' in the 21st Century. The media role in fostering this civic culture on a lifelong basis is of paramount importance for empowering the citizenry to contribute to the institution of values and practices of justice, equality, human rights, gender equality, freedom of expression, and governance in their communities.

The basic 'knowledge society' model provides for the establishment of egalitarian social and economic institutions based on sound democratic values and conventions and an advanced information infrastructure that draws on multiple knowledge-dissemination mechanisms. As noted above, educational and media institutions are the prime components of knowledge building in knowledge societies and their philosophical foundations derive from the very democratic and egalitarian values that define social and political institutions. While an egalitarian milieu is necessary for the democratic functioning of education and media institutions in knowledge societies, those institutions themselves play a significant role in cementing civic culture and fostering mature citizenry in local communities. In this case, the knowledge society model provides for some circular relationships between civic culture disseminating institutions like media and education on the one hand and social, cultural and political institutions, on the other hand. Democratic structures and conventions in knowledge societies play a catalyst role for the institution of civic values though media and education channels while the later furnish the overall culture that sustain the egalitarian system.

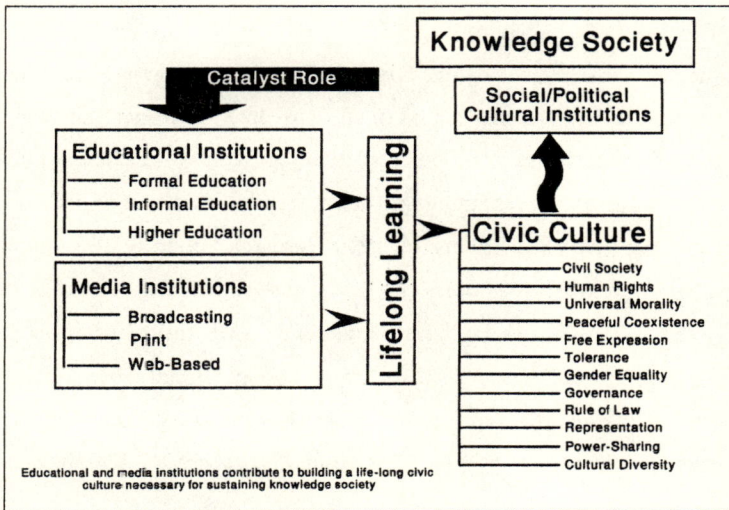

Educational and media institutions contribute to building a life-long civic culture necessary for sustaining knowledge society

The Evolving Arab Communications Scene:
Opportunities & Challenges for Lifelong Civic Education

There is broad consensus among researchers that the face of the Arab World communications landscape has changed significantly over the past two decades (Dubai Press Club, 2008). The information and communications revolution, marked by the introduction of satellite television and the World Wide Web, has induced the proliferation of a greater number of media outlets offering a far more diverse content to an expanding young audience. According to 2008 statistics, there are over 500 satellite television channels available to Arab viewers in the region (ASBU, 2008). Internet penetration rates have reached record levels of 42% in some Arabian Gulf countries, while overall user figures stood at 30 million in 2008 (Internet World Stats, 2008). When combined with a growing mobile telephony sector, communications in the Arab World have developed into prosperous sectors with high attractiveness for both government and commercial operators.

For the first time in the region, broadcasting is no longer a government monopoly as private investments found their way into radio and television operations. Web access has also been a defining feature of the evolving communications scene with emerging applications in education, public relations, journalism, and commerce. According to Madar Research Group (2007), mobile telephony in the Arab World has been one of the fastest-growing sectors in the region, with over 100 million users identified in 2007 (AME Info, 2007). Behind this expanding communications scene lies a growing commercial drive that sees promising profitability in this expanding sector. Recent 2008 data show that advertising spending in the Arab World has reached a record $5 billion, about 70% of it is in the oil-rich Gulf region (Media.ME.com, 2008).

In addition to a growing commercial component, communications developments in the Arab World have also been marked by a relative democratic outlook that enabled broader access to media channels. In the past 10 years, all

Arab societies have experienced some forms of democratic reforms bearing on their social and political systems (Browers, 2006). The initiation of free elections, the establishment of representative bodies, and the institution of legal and constitutional civil reforms have all contributed to the creation of a freer environment for a wide range of formerly disenfranchised individuals and groups (Lynch, 2006). One implication of these developments has been the slow rise of a civil society with varying powers to contest state views and policies. Although some researchers have remained cynical about the power of civil society institutions to stand up to the well-entrenched state power, on certain occasions involving national and regional issues, civil society actors have made strong showings on individual countries' political arenas (Lynch, 2003).

The most outstanding implication of technological, commercial, and political developments has been pertinent to the media sector. It has been noted by some researchers that a new public sphere was in the making in the region as a result of increasing democratization and technological diffusions. According to Lynch (2006), those developments have given rise to new voices in the Arab World, harnessing television channels like *Al Jazeera* and *Al Arabeya* and Web-based media to communicate their unorthodox views on social, political and cultural developments. Ayish (2008) notes that new media outlets have also changed relations with publics who are no longer passive receivers but proactive players in scores of television talk shows and blogs. Media adoption of Western-style journalism has been instrumental in re-defining their role in a traditional state-controlled communications setting where audiences are not expected to contest official views (Ayish, 2001). Providing access to pan-Arab viewers to participate in live talk shows and freely express themselves on controversial political and cultural issues has contributed to the diffusion of a new civic culture in the region. The *Al Jazeera* 'Opposite Direction' program, broadcast over the past 10 years, has included hundreds of episodes on issues like freedom of expression and the press, human rights violations, women rights, corruption, democratization, national identity, globalization, Islamism and others. Viewers were allowed opportunities to comment on debates either through phone call-ins or Internet messages (Zayani, 2005).

The Arab communications landscape is not dominated by a single media paradigm, but by a set of competing models rooted in variant political and social systems. In his survey of journalism models on Arab television, Ayish (2002) identifies three categories of broadcasters: the liberal, the authoritarian, and the mixed. The liberal model is associated with emerging media outlets like *Al Jazeera* and *Al Arabeya* satellite channels, and *Elaph* portal. They also include hundreds of private bloggers with highly critical messages pertaining to the Arab political system. The authoritarian model denotes inherited long-time state-controlled media institutions that have served as mouthpieces for official views. Mixed systems refer to private and state-operated media working side by side under similar legal and regulatory umbrellas. Arab audiences also have access to foreign Arabic-language channels with a liberal discourse like the U.S. *Al Hurra*, the *BBC Arabic Service*, *French 24 Channel*, and *Russia Today*. These channels carry a wide range of political talk shows that draw on democratic discourse to communicate with their audiences. Authoritarian media address democratic issues in local settings only when they are sanctioned by official positions like state-initiated elections or state-inaugurated representative bodies.

The limited number of independent media outlets in the Arab region was bound to have negative implications on civic education. The concept of civic or public media barely exists in mainstream Arab communications and would only be found in emerging fringe Web-based outlets. It is argued that advocacy journalism is an integral feature of Arab communications in the context of government-operated media services which advocate state policies and positions (Awad, 2005). However, this interpretation goes against the essence of this label as referring to detached and objective journalists who do not see any active role in dealing with social and political developments in the community. While government-oriented journalism promotes official policies, advocacy journalism promotes citizens' rights to know and engage in constructive debates bearing on their lives. *Al Jazeera* stands out as the most civic-oriented media in the region despite the fact that other competing media seem to be moving on this direction, yet with support from foreign sides (Miles, 2003).

Implications for Arab Knowledge Societies

The 2008 Arab Cultural Development Report released by the Beirut-based Arab Thought Foundation (Fikr) has offered an assertive account of education and media in the region (Fikr, 2008). The document notes some form of a disconnection between media and educational policies in Arab societies where both sectors are supposed to experience drastic reforms. It was observed that while learning continues to be defined by classical conventions and practices, media policies and regulations have failed to produce a coherent communications system that functions in synch with other knowledge-producing sectors. The same observation was echoed in 2003 in the Arab Human Development Report issued by the UN Development Program on knowledge society conditions in the Arab World (UNDP, 2003). The Report, the most comprehensive document on emerging Arab 'knowledge societies', concludes that knowledge demand, production and dissemination are ineffectual, notwithstanding the abundance of Arab human capital. The document proposes a strategic vision that could support a creative renaissance buttressed by the "five pillars" of an Arab knowledge society which include guaranteeing the key freedoms of opinion, speech and assembly through good governance bounded by the law; disseminating high quality education conducive to a system for life-long learning; indigenizing science, universalizing R&D, and joining the Information Revolution; shifting rapidly towards knowledge-based and value-added production; and developing an authentic, broadminded and enlightened Arab knowledge model.

It is difficult to make a solid claim about any single Arab country attaining the full features of a 'knowledge society'. According to the 2002 and 2003 *Arab Human Development Reports*, key knowledge dissemination processes in Arab countries, (socialization and upbringing, education, the media and translation), face deep-seated social, institutional, economic and political impediments. Notable among these, according to the Reports, are the meager resources available to individuals, families and institutions and the restrictions imposed upon them. The Reports note that impressive gains in the quantitative expansion of education in Arab countries in the last half of the 20th century are still modest in comparison with other developing countries or with the requirements of human development. The Reports' analysis of the status of knowledge in Arab countries indicates the presence of significant human capital that finds refuge in creativity from a restrictive societal and political environment and that could, under favorable circumstances, provide a solid structural foundation for a knowledge renaissance.

The construction of a sustainable knowledge society in the Arab World requires the institution of an advocacy journalism model that fosters civic culture within communities across the region. The two dominant models currently accessible to Arab publics are the authoritarian state model where media are entrusted with official functions and the liberal model in which media practitioners see themselves as independent conduits of information with no mandate to go beyond their professionally-inscribed objectivity. If knowledge society is about human development, then new traditions of journalism such as development journalism, emancipator journalism, and public or civic journalism, should be considered to achieve that goal (Sakr, 2007). State media are not expected to push for community engagement in public life beyond the classical mobilization function to rally the masses around government initiatives.

On the other hand, the few media outlets with Western-style orientations in the region seem either inhibited by professional cannons of journalism or by repressive state policies. It is for this reason that new media outlets that depend on independent initiatives hold a better promise for citizens' empowerment in public community affairs. In Egypt, bloggers played a central role in motivating voters to go to the polls in local elections and in exposing cases of rigging and corruption (Levinson, 2005). *Al Jazeera Satellite Channel* has devoted extensive coverage to national elections in several Arab countries in addition to live coverage of civil society events pertaining to freedom of expression globalization, women rights, Islamist perspectives, and constitutional reforms.

The role of public media in advocating civic consciousness in emerging knowledge societies in the Arab World is likely to remain a function of future political and social developments. In the 1990s, some Western scholars spoke of the 'Arab Street' as a potential force to be reckoned with in affecting change in the region (Pollock, 1992). But as Ayish (2008) points out, the notion of the 'Arab Street' has remained amore a vision than a real phenomenon often stifled by heightened state authoritarianism, global power pragmatism, Islamic fundamentalism and socio-cultural underdevelopment. The search for a more independent media system in the region has often been associated with the search for appropriate social and political recipes to address its deep-running woes. It is for this reason also that the concept of knowledge society would continue to be more of an aspired goal than of a tangible reality in a region with over 70 million illiterates that compound serious social, political, and economic problems facing Arab societies.

A Case in Point: Al-Jazeera Network as a Civic Media Institution

Al-Jazeera Satellite Channel (JSC) was launched in 1997 from Qatar in the aftermath of the discontinuation of a *BBC Arabic Satellite Channel*'s joint venture with Saudi-owned *Orbit Television and Radio Network*. Over the past few years, JSC has presented itself as a forum for "the Opinion and the Other Opinion." Funded by advertising revenue and subsidies from the Government of Qatar, JSC has marked a major transition in Arab world broadcast media with its critical talk shows and live coverage of regional and global events. The channel's critical reporting of domestic political and religious affairs in several Arab countries has led to a series of diplomatic incidents as well as to the closure of some of its offices abroad (Da Lage, 2005: 56). The channel's bold approach to political issues and developments has also generated misgivings about its journalistic performance (Hudson, 2006). By late 2008, *Al Jazeera Arabic Satellite Channel* has become just one service operating within *Al Jazeera Network*, an umbrella organization housing an English channel, a documentary channel, a children's channel, a sports channel, a direct broadcast channel, an online website, and a human rights and liberties department.

Regardless of the controversies surrounding *Al Jazeera*, it is inarguable that the network has brought about a dramatic transformation in the long-stagnant Arab World media sphere. Lynch (2004)) notes that *Al Jazeera* has presented itself as an alternative to state-run television, providing a forum for political views that are not likely to be positively received by government-operated media in the Arab World. He cited the example of the pre-eminent Egyptian journalist Muhammad Hassanayn Haykal who was summarily banned in the spring 2004 from appearing on Egyptian television after he broached the deeply sensitive topic of Gamal Mubarak's aspirations to succeed his father as president. In response to the ban, Haykal signed a blockbuster deal with *Al-Jazeera*, to air a weekly show entitled "With Haykal: A Life Experience," devoting the first episode of the show to exposing the Egyptian government's efforts to silence his dissent. From Lynch's point of view, the experience of the venerable Haykal demonstrates how, by shattering state control over public debate, Arab satellite television "is building the foundation of a more democratic Arab political culture" (Lynch, 2004).

Al-Jazeera Satellite Channel, as a new media phenomenon in the Arab World, has attracted a wide range of research, seeking to investigate how this pan-Arab television channel contributes to the transformation of the traditionally state-controlled media environment. Miles (2003) notes that as a result of *Al-Jazeera*'s critique of many Arab governments, Arab television has been labeled by some observers as a virtual "political party". But he remarks that media can surely not compensate for the lack of civil society organization and the weakness of the existing opposition. Another volume edited by Zayani (2005) took a more critical approach to *Al-Jazeera* while recognizing its impressive contributions to the emerging Arab public sphere in the area. Zayani notes that in spite of its relatively short history, this Qatar-based news network seems to have left an indelible mark in the Arab world that has changed the face of the otherwise parochial Arab media - although in the West, it is largely perceived as a channel that is set on countering Western ideologies.

In an earlier book on *JSC* El-Nawawy and Iskander (2002) also spoke lyrically of the channel's pro-democratization orientations in the Arab region and its role in pre-empting traditional Arab state media censorship by providing alternative perspectives on issues relating to politics, religion, and other sensitive cultural aspects of contemporary Arabian societies. Both authors noted that the Qatar-based television network has been a hugely positive force in the Middle East "because it has put pressure on authoritarian Arab regimes and helped to promote freedom of expression." According to the two authors, the network differs from Western news networks because it has an "Arab perspective,' they say, but this does not make it any more biased than American networks that have an "American perspective.'

The channel's newscasts, political and cultural talk shows and documentaries provide the staple for its daily programming to global audiences inside the Arab World and beyond. There are regular newscasts carried at the top of the hour, in addition to three major news round-up programs in the morning, at noon and at midnight.

The channel maintains a huge network of correspondents covering almost all Arab countries and major world capitals. In addition, the channel draws on a wide range of political and cultural talk shows, the most imminent of which are "Opposite Direction," a Cross-Fire style political show; "More Than One Opinion," a live talk program in which studio and remote-site guests are engaged; and "Without Frontiers," a Hard-Talk style show in which one personality is interviewed with audience call-in feedback. Other programs include "al-Jazeera Forum" which discusses an important topic with full audience participation; "Open Dialogue" which is town-hall style show on selected topics, and "Behind the News" which is a 30-minute nightly discussion of an important issue arising in the context of local, national or international developments.

The channel also runs a news text strip carrying the main headlines that are updated when necessary to keep audiences abreast of regional and global news developments. JSC Direct also carries coverage of civil society events like demonstrations, seminars, speeches, and developing stories while its documentary channel broadcasts a wide range of programs on past and current Arab politics and society. *Al Jazeera Network* is made up of four channels: News, Satellite Channel, Knowledge, Business, and Liberties and Human Rights. The latter service was inaugurated in November 2008 to commemorate the release of *JSC* cameraman Sami al Haji who was appointed head of the new section.

Al Jazeera Network's contributions to civic culture in the Arab World may need a full-fledged research project to unravel its different dimensions. But based on systematic observations of those services, this writer has identified the following areas of civic empowerment offered by the Network:

-Providing a voice for disenfranchised citizens across the Arab World to express their views on a wide range of political and social issues. This feature flows from *JSC*'s declared philosophy of giving time and space for 'opinion and counter opinion.' Arabs have become able to post their feedback to evolving issues and developments on Aljazeera.net and to air them on *JSC*'s live talk shows like 'Opposite Direction,' 'More Than One Opinion,' 'Al

Jazeera Forum,' and 'Open Dialogue' in addition to interviews hosted on *JSC*'s Direct Channel.

-Providing a venue of expression for alternative political and social perspectives that may not be compatible with mainstream Arab World views through hosting personalities on the different shows and providing space for their contributions to the Network's portal.

-Setting a civic public agenda for Arab society through playing up issues and topics compatible with democratic conventions like human rights, elections, constitutional amendments, women equality, and freedom of expression, cultural identity, religious fanaticism, interfaith dialogue, corruption, representation, political repression and others.

-Furnishing extensive coverage and analysis to civic events and developments as evident in dispatching a special crew to cover elections in Kuwait, Yemen, Bahrain, Mauritania, Jordan, and Palestine. *JSC*'s Direct Channel also carries live or pre-recorded coverage of civic events by civil society actors like protest rallies, parliamentary sessions, elections, speeches, seminars and others.

-Adopting a civic media discourse that boils down to respecting citizens' rights to free expression and participation in decision making at different levels.

-Exposing the tragic faces of international power pragmatism through shedding light on Western support for Israeli aggression as well as for political despotism in the region.

Conclusion and Summary

Media have always been viewed not only as powerful channels of communication, but also as lifelong learning tools that contribute to defining public consciousness about a wide range of issues. Researchers have established that media, especially those emerging in the past two decades, perform functions that go beyond the mere delivery of impartial information to audiences; they also take proactive roles in stimulating further community engagement in political processes and in constructing sound and sustainable civic consciousness among the citizenry. The rise of civic journalism in the United States in the late 1980s marked a departure from mainstream professional media conventions that prescribed a detached and objective role for journalists in community life. By enhancing citizens' awareness of civic features of their contemporary life, media would contribute to the perpetuation of moral human values of social justice and democratic governance which are central pillars of knowledge societies. In this lifelong learning process, citizens are exposed to media content that promotes civil society values embracing human rights gender equality, democratic representation and fee expression.

This advocacy media role in the Arab World has been rather less visible in the region's public life. A convergence of social, political economic and professional factors seemed to have militated against the institution of civic journalism as an enduring feature of the Arab communications landscape. State authoritarianism, coupled with global power pragmatism, Western-style journalism, and cultural underdevelopment has precluded the emergence of alternative media orientations with explicit civic functions. However the evolving Arab public sphere has witnessed the birth of new media outlets that mark a break away from mainstream communications traditions. *Al Jazeera Network* and a wide range of blogger sites have provided Arab populations with fresh and less fettered opportunities for expression.

Given the fact that civic education is a long-term process spanning full generations, it is clear that the new media, along with reformed educational systems, are potential forces in the drive for the institution of civic culture. But we have to remember that public media alone cannot bring about the democratic transitions needed for sustaining the type of civic culture needed for the development of a knowledge society. Media cannot perform their civic lifelong learning role in the absence of solid constitutional and political arrangements that promote the diffusion and adoption of civic practices.

References and Notes

AME Info. (2007). Madar Research forecasts 109 million Arab mobile subscriptions by 2008, at : http://www.ameinfo.com/69154.html.

Arab States Broadcasting Union (2008). Description of the current situation of Arab satellite channels,' at: http://www.asbu.net/www/en/doc.asp?mcat=5&mrub=33.

Ayish, M. (2001). American-style journalism and Arab World television: An exploratory study of news selection at six Arab world satellite television channels,' *Transnational Broadcasting Journal.* No. 6, Spring\summer at: http://www.tbsjournal.com/Archives/Spring01/Ayish.html.

(2002). Political communication on Arab world television: Evolving patterns. *Political Communication.* No. (19): 137-154.

(2008). *The new Arab public sphere.* Berlin: Frank & Timme.

Bird, E., Lutz, R. and Warick, C. (2008). Media as partners in education for sustainable development: A training and resource kit. UNESCO Series on Journalism Education. Paris: UNESCO Publishing.

Bowers, J. (1993). *American Stories: Case Studies in Government and Politics.* Belmont, CA: Wadsworth Publishing Company.

Bowers, J. Claflin, B. and Walker, G. (1998). A case study from Rochester, New York: The impact of civic journalism projects on voting behavior in state-wide referendums, a paper presented at the Annual Meeting of the New England Political Science Association, May 1-2, Worcester, MA.

Browers, M. (2006). *Democracy and civil society in Arab political thought: Trans-cultural possibilities.* New York: Syracuse University Press.

Cecchini, M. (2003). Active citizenship, adult learning and active citizenship, lifelong learning and active citizenship, Key note speech.EAEA Conference, Nicosia, Cyprus, 15 November.

Cogan, J. (1998). Citizenship education for the 21st century: Setting the context,' in Cogan, J. & Derricott, R. (eds), *Citizenship for the 21st century: An international perspective on education,* London, Kogan Page.

Da Lage, O. (2005). The politics of Al Jazeera or the diplomacy of Doha, in Zayani, M. (ed.), *Al Jazeera phenomenon: Critical perspectives on new Arab media.* New York: Pluto Press.

Daniel, W. (2006). Lifelong learning of the future: A vision, a paper presented at the *Roundtable on Learning from the Past to Build the Future,* European Schoolnet, Burgess, Belgium, Dec. 7-8.

Denton, F. and Thorson, E. (1994). 'Civic journalism; Does it work? A special report for the Pew Center for Civic Journalism on the "We the People" project,' Madison, Wis.

Dubai Press Club. (2008). *Arab media outlook: 2008-2012.* London: Price Water House Coopers.

El-Nawawi, M. and A. Iskander. (2003). *Al-Jazeera: How the free Arab news network scooped the world and changed the Middle East.* Cambridge, MA: Westview.

Fales, A. W. (1996). Lifespan learning development, 183-187. In Colin J.T. (ed.) *Lifelong education for adults: An international handbook.* Pergamon Press.

Fikr (Arab Thought Foundation). (2008). *Arab cultural development report*. Beirut: Fikr
    Publishing.
Flannigan, W. and Zingale, N. (1994). *Political behavior of the American electorate*.
    Washington, D.C.: CQ Press.
Fretwell, D. and Colombano, J. (2000). *Emerging policies and programs for the 21st century in
    upper and middle income countries*. Washington, D. C.: World Bank.
Friedland, L. (2002). Measuring civic journalism's progress: A report across a decade of activity, a
    study conducted for the Pew Center for Civic Journalism.
Hudson, M. (2006). Washington and AlJazeera: Face to face: Competitive structures to create
    Middle East realities, in Emirates Center for Strategic Studies and Research (ECSSR),
    Arab media in the information age conference proceedings. Abu Dhabi: ECSSR, pp. 243-
    266.
Istance, D. (2008). Lifelong learning and citizenship: International perspectives,' in Williams, E.
    and Humphreys, G. (eds.) *Citizenship education and lifelong learning: Power and place*.
    New York: Nova Press.
Internet World Stats. (2008). Internet usage in the Middle East: Middle East internet usage &
    population statistics. At : http://www.internetworldstats.com/.
Levinson, C. (2005). Egypt's growing blogger community pushes limit of dissent. *The Christian
    Science Monitor*, August 24, p. 6.
Longworth, N. (2002). *Making lifelong learning work: Learning cities for a learning century*.
    New York: Routledge.
Lynch, M. (2003). Beyond the Arab street: Iraq and the Arab public sphere, *Politics & Society*,
    31(1) pp. 55-91.
Lynch, M. (2004). Shattering the politics of silence: Satellite television talk shows and the
    transformation of Arab political culture,' *Arab Reform Bulletin*, December 2004, Volume
    2, Issue 11, at:
    http://www.carnegieendowment.org/publications/index.cfm?fa=view&id=16242.
Lynch, M. (2006). *Voices of the new Arab public: Iraq, al-Jazeera, and Middle East politics
    today*. New York: Columbia University Press.
Mansell, R. and Wehn, U. (1998). *Knowledge societies: Information technology for sustainable
    development*. New York, United Nations Commission on Science and Technology for
    Development/Oxford University Press.
McIntosh, C. (2005). Introduction, in McIntosh, C. and Z. Varoglu. *Perspectives on distance
    education: Lifelong learning and distance higher education*. Paris: UNESCO Publishing.
Media.ME.com. (2008). GCC media corners $3.7bn of advertising spend, against $733m for the
    entire Levant region. At: http://mediame.com/taxonomy/tags/pan_arab_research_center
Miles, H. (2003). *Al Jazeera: The inside story of the Arab news channel that is challenging the
    West*. London: Grove Press.
Moreno, J. (2005). *Learning to teach in the knowledge society: Final report*, World Bank,
    Washington, D. C.
Awad, A. (2005). Online journalism in the Arab world. *Proceedings of the conference on online
    journalism in the Arab world*, University of Sharjah, UAE, Nov. 5-6.
Pew Center for Civic Journalism .(2008). At: http://www.pewcenter.org/doingcj/.
Pollock, D. (1992). *The Arab street: Public opinion in the Arab world*. Washington, D. C.: The
    Washington Institute.
Ranney, Austin. (1983). *Channels Of power*. New York: Basic Books.
Rogers, E. (2003). *Diffusion of innovations*. New York, NY: Free Press.
Sakr, N. (2007). *Arab television today*. London: Tauris Publishers.
Schaffer, J. (2004). 'The Role of newspapers in building citizenship,' keynote speech at 5th
    Brazilian Newspaper Congress, São Paulo, Brazil, September 13, 2004.
UNDP. (2003). *Arab human development report: Building a knowledge society*. New York:
    UNDP Publishing.

UNESCO. (2004). *Learning: The treasure within*. Paris: UNESCO Publishing.
UNESCO. (2005). *Towards knowledge societies*. Paris: UNESCO Publishing.
World Bank. (2003). *Lifelong learning in the global knowledge economy: Challenges for developing countries*. Washington, D. C.: World Bank.
Yankelovich, D. (1991). *Coming to public judgment*. Syracuse, NY: Syracuse University Press.
Zayani, M. (2005). *The Al Jazeerah phenomenon*. Boulder, CO: Paradigm Publishers.

Chapter Three

Using Campus Media to Mentally Position Students for the Emerging Media Delivery Systems

Joel R. Willer
University of Louisiana at Monroe

Although student-produced campus media outlets have long existed in various forms on college and university campuses, a great variety has existed in how individual campuses have in the past implemented student media. Therefore, as traditional student media now transform to serve within the new communication frontier created by emerging delivery systems, they face the challenge of arriving at an uncertain destination starting from very divergent points of beginning.

For the purpose of this discussion, traditional student media include newspaper, yearbook, magazine, radio and television. Within each of these categories the specific implementation of student media on different campuses is shaped by a number of factors. For instance, some traditional student media are administratively housed within a closely related academic program such as communication, journalism, or mass communications; others are housed within academic programs less specific to media, such as within an English department; and still others are administered outside any academic program, such as a student life department. Various student media are sometimes situated under dissimilar organizational structures on the same campus: a campus newspaper might publish from within a journalism program, but the radio station on the same campus might be a "club" answering to student life. Indeed, one standard of the Accrediting Council on Education in Journalism and Mass Communications requires that institutions with an accredited academic unit "provide students with extra-curricular activities and opportunities that are relevant to the curriculum and develop their professional as well as intellectual abilities and interests" (ACEJMC, 2007, p. 48); however, ACEJMC does not require such extra-curricular activities to be housed within the accredited unit, only that the *institution* provide these opportunities. As traditional student media increasingly converge to adapt to new delivery systems, institutions must evaluate historical organizational arrangements and remove any structural barriers that might inhibit students from participating across media platforms.

Individual Medium in a Global Environment

There is no doubt that developments in global communication technologies have impacted the ways in which individual users designed their content. These developments have also influenced organizational and institutional decisions. This chapter has demonstrated how student media in the United States transformed to serve within the new communication frontier created by emerging delivery systems. Hence, the intended purpose of an individual student medium – for the students producing material for that medium – might also vary from institution to institution, or even between media at the same institution. Some student media are intended to offer pre-professional preparation for students ultimately pursuing careers in media – often these are the student media structurally organized under an academic program and are closely aligned with the formal curriculum. Other student media are intended solely to provide participating students with a creative outlet, with no intention of providing deliberate preparation for aspiring media professionals. Student media organized within student life programs are most often intended for this second purpose, as are some media operated within an academic unit. Student media designated to enhance professional preparation have a more immediate need to embrace the emerging delivery systems in order to prepare graduates for the certain change occurring in the greater media environment. Although somewhat less urgent, even those student media that do not aspire to prepare media professionals will need to adapt to emerging delivery systems in order to remain relevant to media consumers – higher education demographics, thus the campus media audience, include a high concentration of new media early adopters.

Even the so-called traditional student media are at times characterized by their use of non-conventional delivery systems. Student "radio" stations on many campuses are not heard on over-the-air broadcast frequencies, oftentimes because of a lack of available licensed spectrum, but might make use of an unlicensed transmission, a spare channel on a cable television system, or a closed public address system. Student television stations are most often not over-the-air broadcasts, but are usually carried on cable systems. Student television enterprises might include a regular schedule of daily or weekly programs, or might be limited to the occasional recorded or live program. Student newspapers might publish daily, weekly, biweekly or some other intermittent schedule. Long before recent discussions about media convergence, many college and university yearbooks remade themselves as periodic magazines in order to remain pertinent to contemporary readers. Existing delivery systems used by student media will certainly factor in to any transition to new distribution channels.

New Communication Frontiers

The new communication frontier is now in the continuing process of discovery and colonization by academics, students, and media professionals alike. The related buzzword "convergence" has many potential meanings, the complete exploration of which is far beyond the scope of this discussion; however, on its most basic level the term implies a coming together. For student media, that coming together represents crossing the boundaries which have historically separated the traditional mass communications outlets to present information and entertainment using an assortment of media. On a slightly more advanced level, convergence includes the delivery of content outside its traditional delivery platform. Here, student media are likely to port material – including repurposed versions of the same content previously produced for traditional media – to the Internet and to emergent portable electronic media. Our developing comprehension of the phenomenon also leads us to recognize an even more advanced level of convergence, where the role of the audience changes from the linear nature we have previously known, now allowing consumers to self-direct content delivery, interact, and even generate mass media content. At this heightened level student media creators must make the most radical adjustment in how they produce and manage content.

In many ways, instead of being future-thinkers, the academy is now playing catch-up with media convergence as it has been developing in the professional world,. Student media can provide the venue to experiment with the application of new technologies and methods of producing media content. Much of what is necessary to facilitate this pioneering effort involves changing the mindset of the student media participants. A number of campuses in the United States have embarked on efforts to create converged media. Such efforts often begin with structural changes, such as moving parts of formerly separate media operations into common physical workspace. Kent State University's School of Journalism and Mass Communications recently moved into a renovated building that includes a consolidated newsroom. Though the Kent State student media share physical space, respective media retain traditional organizational structures. 'The converged newsroom will give student media more opportunities to work together as one news organization – that's the biggest benefit to both us and the student body,' says Rachel Abbey, editor of the Fall 2007 *Daily Kent Stater*. 'Being in one room, we will literally be able to sit next to one another and work on stories together'" (Compton, 2008). However, merely locating print, radio, and television journalists in a joint workspace does not automatically create a "converged" newsroom.

Journalism is inherently about competition, not cooperation. A key student mindset to first strive to change is to transform the former sense of competition into one of cooperation. Further structural reforms to consider include developing an umbrella identity to unify former adversaries. An example of such a creation is "i-Comm" at Brigham Young University. "A rapidly changing industry has made necessary the birth of a new creation in the Communication Department. i-Comm, a convergence of student-led media groups, is a way for students from many academic majors to use their skills in practical and professionally modeled ways" (Nguyen, 2007). The use of such an enveloping identity need not necessarily replace the names of traditional outlets; such a drastic implementation risks alienating staff members and audience alike. The crucial point is to create common ground and common cause. Likewise, if the respective media retain vestiges of former internal organizational structures, the emotional boundaries are also likely to remain. For example, if the goal is to construct a joint news operation consideration might be given to reformation of the editorial chain of command so that one individual is responsible for story assignments for all outlets: print, broadcast, and online.

A benefit of fostering new forms of cooperation is that strengths of individual staff members can be combined in complementary ways, allowing for the more effective telling of stories. Converged media provide multiple means for storytelling. Various elements of the same story might be best told using the printed word, video, or interactive graphics. Jeff Schenck, the UCLA *Daily Bruin* editor, stresses the use of media appropriate to the story. "'All stories are different, and it takes different media to cover them properly,' Schenck concludes. 'A red-carpet thing doesn't work well in print, so we cover it in video now. The Regents approving something can't be covered well on video, but we are doing that in print. It's even wrong to call it a paper: It's a news source now'" (Greenberg, 2007).

Online editions of many newspapers, including some student newspapers, have already embraced video components to supplement text versions of stories. Early examples of such efforts have been the less-than-polished creations of print journalists without formal training in videography and video editing; increased production values are obviously more likely through cooperation between traditional print and video outlets, where journalists with pertinent training produce the respective media content. Jason Brummond, the editor-in-chief of the *Daily Iowan* at the University of Iowa works with television journalists to bring video into the online edition of the newspaper. "'The hardest thing has been getting people to work together,' Brummond said. 'In newspapers, people have identified themselves as a print journalist or a broadcast journalist.... The biggest challenge is getting those people to work on the same story, go out together and cover an event'" (Pesce, 2008). Developing student buy-in can include the satisfaction gained through collaborative successes.

Fostering unity also requires the developing of respect for inherent differences between the traditional media aspects of the newly cooperative entities. Traditional print outlets such as newspapers and magazines are almost exclusively rooted in journalistic content, while the traditional electronic outlets of radio and television include combinations of journalistic and non-journalistic entertainment content. Many early convergence efforts in student media have focused primarily on journalistic content alone, which naturally leads to resistance from students principally interested in the neglected non-journalistic matter. An example of this point might be that the traditional role of a student radio station has been the presentation of music strictly as entertainment, while the traditional role of a student newspaper might have included a critical review of a newly-released music recording; the converged online outlet should not be limited to a rehashed version of the print review, but might include *both* the review and presentation of the music recording itself, or a portion thereof.

Initial forays by student media into new delivery systems are frequently limited to retransmitting content originally produced for traditional media through a new channel – most often, the Internet. Such efforts might include the cooperation across traditional media platforms discussed above, but often they do not. The student newspaper creates a Web site, branded to match the traditional print edition, which simply repeats verbatim content from the print edition. The student over-the-air radio station creates its own Web site, through which it provides basic information describing the station and, most importantly, adds a live audio stream comprised of the same programming distributed to its broadcast transmitter. In other cases, where a broadcast frequency is not available, an Internet-only station is created that mimics the programming of a traditional student radio station. Like the student radio station, the student television station creates a Web site describing the station and providing an additional outlet for stored video files of programs previously distributed through more traditional channels. The common factor in each of these examples is that minimal effort is necessary to create an online presence. An important mindset to address in each of these examples is students' tendency to view the online version as an afterthought – *first*, the traditional media is produced, *and then* comes the Internet version. The print edition of the newspaper is viewed as *the* product and the online edition is lagniappe; the print edition *must* be put out by deadline, but the online edition might succumb to staff fatigue and might get updated, or not – particularly if the newspaper has only a small staff. Likewise, radio and television Web sites are allowed to become woefully outdated due to the day-to-day demands and distraction of producing for the traditional outlets.

Traditional Media v. New Media

Though repurposing tradition media content to the new media can be efficient use of resources, it does not necessarily maximize the potential of the new outlets. A student newspaper Web site provides the opportunity to present timely information between printed editions or to provide in-depth coverage not possible in a space-limited print edition. A student radio station Web site could recap entire daily playlists to help audience members accurately identify music of interest, or could provide extended artist profiles too detailed to present in the related broadcast. A television Web site might provide the synopsis of episode plotlines for a student-produced serial drama. Again, by collaboratively working together student media practitioners across platforms can provide content superior to individual efforts in the traditional media. Students must be encouraged to consider the additional potential of the new media channels, and to not view them merely as extending the reach of traditional media.

At the opposite extreme, naïveté might lead a hasty conclusion that new media outlets can or will soon supplant traditional outlets. Case in point is the announcement by the president of Chattanooga State Community College of the sale of the license for broadcast radio station WAWL, to be replaced with a Web-only station (Courter, March 19, 2008). The explanations for the decision ignore the fact that Internet radio is not yet as portable as broadcast radio. A cost-saving justification does not consider that streaming costs per listener do not scale the same as for broadcast stations – each additional online listener significantly increases costs, while additional broadcast listeners do not – and that an online station with an audience comparable to a broadcast counterpart would be prohibitively expensive. A cited benefit of migration to Web-only distribution is a potential for online archiving of programming – proposed in a manner specifically in violation of the federal copyright statute. The Chattanooga State president also stated, "I believe it (a digital radio mandate) is coming, but also we are dedicated to doing things right, and for a radio station that plays music that would mean going digital" (Courter, March 28, 2008), a statement that does not square with the fact that a Web-only radio station performing music will provide lesser audio quality than the predecessor analog broadcast outlet – many people mistakenly confuse "digital" Internet transmissions with "perfect copy." The predicted demise of traditional media is, for now, premature.

Legal Challenges

The new delivery systems add legal challenges that student content producers must consider, particularly in the area of intellectual property. The Webcasting of commercially released recorded music triggers complex statutory content requirements along with new performance royalties. Podcasts containing music are subject to copyright limitations not applicable to either Webcasts or to over-the-air transmissions. Web sites incorporating blogs and discussion forums raise additional legal and policy issues regarding the potential editing of content. Changes in technology initially disrupt customary ways of accomplishing tasks. Students engaged in campus media must get used to doing things differently. The best way to facilitate this type of transition is to not only provide the tools, but to also ensure that abundant training is provided in order to minimize anxiety. Students need to be made aware that at the outset the commitment of additional time will be necessary to accomplish even familiar tasks utilizing new technologies – something that proves challenging within tight student schedules – but as the learning curve eventually flattens productivity ultimately should be enhanced.

The importance to student media of convergence and the evolving delivery systems extends beyond training practitioners to work in more than one of the traditional media, but also includes preparation for storytelling in a new media form yet to be fully developed and serving audiences consuming media in new ways. Students must be focused on the message, not on the production platform. Now it is more important than has always been the case that students need to be made to regard the technology as tools used to communicate a message. Media consumers are increasingly platform agnostic, gathering information across different media platforms. Student media practitioners must be similarly broadminded, otherwise they risk losing reader, viewer, and listener attention to competing outlets.

Conclusion and Summary

Emerging delivery systems are also changing the relationships between media senders and receivers, as the Facebook and YouTube generation increasingly expects to be engaged in interactive communication, including by means of consumer-produced content. Student media producers as media consumers are themselves part of the group of most intense participants in these developments, and they should be first reminded to incorporate the experience of their personal media utilization patterns into their own decisions and secondly need to be encouraged to experiment with new forms of discourse. A panelist speaking during the University of Tennessee Student Media Convergence Week recently reiterated this point: "Benz pointed out an advantage the current generation of college students has: familiarity with the online world. Using Facebook, Flicker and YouTube is second nature to college students, which are valuable skills in the new world of online journalism" (Petrie, 2008).

As content choices increase for media consumers, student media producers must also consider how to expedite the filtering of daunting amounts of information. Conventional wisdom posits that media consumers crave an infinitely expansive choice of media content; however, it is much more likely that consumers truly desire expedient fulfillment of their information needs. Victory goes to the media outlet that most expeditiously provides the material the consumer seeks.

Though most everyone acknowledges the need for student media to embrace convergence and emerging delivery systems, students often become reticent when actually faced with change. Some of that reluctance is easily attributed to the fact that this particular change has an uncertain endpoint. Further apprehension is caused by the need to break down established territorialism.

Learning innovative technologies and embracing new communications processes provide further challenges for students' acceptance of change. Ultimately, this evolution provides the potential to more effectively communicate with the student media audiences, and to thereby maintain relevance within the campus communities.

References and Notes

Accrediting Council on Education in Journalism and Mass Communications (2001). *Journalism and Mass Communications Accreditation 2007-2008.*

Compton, M. (Spring 2008). One Newsroom Fits All. *Jargon* Vol. LXIX (Issue 1), 24-28.

Courter, B. (March 19, 2008). Chattanooga State Radio Station Going Online; Tower, License To Be Sold. *Chattanooga Times Free Press.* Retrieved
March 20, 2008 from http://chattan.com/articles/article_124219.asp.

Courter, B. (March 28, 2008). Courter: Clearing the air regarding WAWL's sale. *Chattanooga Times Free Press.* Retrieved March 31, 2008 from http://timesfreepress.com/news/2008/mar/28/courter-clearing-air-regarding-wawls-sale/.
Greenberg, B. (2007). Paper Trails: How the Daily Bruin Became a Training Ground for Leadership and One of the Best-Known College Newspapers in America. *UCLA.*

Magazine Online. Retrieved March 24, 2008 from http://www.magazine.ucla.edu/features/daily-bruin-newspaper/index.html.

Nguyen, P. (October 2, 2007). i-Comm Student Media: New student media organization, i-Comm, aims to give communication students up-to-date real-world experience. *Scroll Online.* Retrieved March 24, 2008 from http://www.byui.edu/scroll/campus/2007/10/20071002-i-comm-student media. htm.

Pesce, A. (January 23, 2008). Convergence makes headlines for collegiate publications. *The Daily Bruin.* Retrieved March 24, 2008 from http://www.dailybruin.ucla.edu/news/ 2008/jan/23/convergence-makes-headlines-collegiate-publication/.

Petrie, S. and Farima, A. (February 21, 2008). Panelists give insight into online journalism.*Tennessee Journalist.* Retrieved March 24, 2008 from http://tnjn.com/2008/feb/21/ panelists-give-insight-into-on/.

Chapter Four

Arab Citizen Journalism Shaped by New Media Technologies Creates A Challenge to Mainstream Media, Authorities and Media Laws

Naila Hamdy
American University in Cairo

This chapter presents a qualitative assessment of citizen journalism and activism efforts throughout the Middle Eastern region in the last few years by shedding light on the technologies accessed and used and the results of specific efforts. Using technology determinism theories to frame this empowerment, it examines the unique qualities of these technologies that allow for an environment of carte blanche communication expressions, mobilization, and citizen story telling bringing more democracy and civic engagement to the region. It also shows the interconnection between global and regional development through the lens of global communication.

Arab citizens looking for methods to mobilize support for their ideas and to influence others and to pressure governments with their demands and their opinions have harnessed new communication technologies to disseminate their journalism and activism. This choice has resulted in fundamental transformations in mainstream media agendas and has caused a shift in government response toward them.

Fueled by technologies that have been noted to promote democracy and social change in an increasingly globalized world marked with interconnected communication networks (Castells 2008), these citizen journalists were initially triggered by the divisive 2004 war in Iraq to disseminate their communicative expressions. Using news websites, discussion bulletins, internet groups, and emails, Arabs in and out of the region could discuss, editorialize and argue about the war. (Hamdy & Mobarak, Iraq War Ushers in Web-Based Era, 2004) In a similar fashion to their global counterparts Arabs also quickly took to the open source technology of blogs to post their stories and commentaries immediately challenging both the static fare provided by mainstream media and government restrictions. (Levinson, 2005) Naturally their efforts did not stop at blogging but have spread to YouTube, Facebook, and Twitter. (Fam, 2008) In addition, with the great expansion of mobile technology, citizens were further empowered to blog from their phones, take pictures and videos to add to their messages. (UAE most wired country in the Arab world, 2008) Arab citizens have been consciously using these new technologies as they emerge to fill the void created by media's ignoring of important events and issues as media outlets have been disconnected themselves from the public needs for many years. Arab citizens have also used these technologies to spawn activist movements and ideologies, including the propagation of radicalized Islam. The questions to be answered by this chapter are whether the availability of these technologies created their behavior, whether these participants have been able to impact mainstream media in the Middle East in general and the Arab world in particular, and how they are perceived by governments. The following pages examine how existing media laws fail to address rights of citizen journalists. Finally, the study will attempt to evaluate the link between digital technologies and the democratization process in the region.

Background

It is believed that new technologies like satellite television and the internet have played a democratizing function and have helped in establishing a civil society in the Arab world. The literature suggests that many of these changes can be attributed to a swift and dramatic change in the media landscape. The Arab satellite revolution with its liberating force may have had most of the focus of media scholars; however, the Internet too has been seen as a medium that is likely to have profound implications for democratization in the region. (Annabelle, 2001; Sakr, 2001; El-Nawawy & Iskandar, 2002) In fact, there is a clear show of determinism that is part of the overflow of enthusiasm and optimism about new communication technology and democratic participation in a debate originating in the West. Digital interactive media is seen as a vehicle for citizen participation in the democratic process. The Internet is touted for that capacity because of its choice of open architecture which contrasts to earlier traditional communications media with their limitations. For that reason the internet allows for diversity of opinion, ideas, and information, setting the ground for more grassroots discourse. It also allows for more complete information which is a corner stone of democracy. Added bonuses are the relatively low barriers to entry, the possibility of many to many communication, and its decentralized organization, all collectively leading to this utopian vision. (Berman & Daniel, 1997)

Technological Determinism

Many discussions of the Internet center on technological determinism or the notion that technology leads to social change. This change refers to both increased democracy and implicit increased freedom. (Barlow, 1996) In fact several technological optimists such as Bell (1973), Barber (1984), and Toffler (1980) have already asserted that with the onset of the information society the Internet has the potential to enhance democratic practices. Following its public availability in the 1990's enthusiasts viewed these emerging technologies as able to create a return to the direct democracy of ancient Greece. (Gilder, 1992; Rheingold, 1992/2000).

In turn because of the global nature of the internet it is assumed by technological determinists that the same principle can apply globally. Conversely, critics contend that the advent of new digital technologies are only automating existing democracy rather than enabling such social changes. Others believe that technology may even exacerbate obstacles that already exist. (Walton, 2007;

Sparks C., 2005) Other researchers argue that the Internet remains in control of powerful groups and some argue for revisiting previous Internet organization's jurisdictions. (Schiller, 1996; Lips & Jaap, 2005) These critics may have a good argument, none the less, the case has been made that the Internet does at least give the voiceless a voice. For instance, one message on a blog can be magnified multiple times if the audience find it relevant. In fact with the increase of wireless mobile devices Joi Ito makes the argument that this will boost "moblogging," that is, posting pictures, videos and texts from mobile phones and the use of wikis - a track back weblog, and that these tools may enable a higher-level order that can help create an emergent democracy that the world needs more than ever. (Ito, 2003) Yes, blogs have had political power, cell phones have been used to organize opposition, and internet connections have been problematic to monitor; however, it is arguable whether this increase in the free flow of information afforded by these technologies has had any real impact on authoritarian regimes. There are anecdotal examples to illustrate both sides of this coin. There are incidents such as the Ukrainian "Orange Revolution" when rigged elections were reversed but on the other hand there are governments such as that of China that succeeded in intimidating Google to comply with their policies. (Walton, 2007) Certainly the Arab region has had its share of notable blogging, mobilizing, text messaging, twittering, and Facebook activism that has not gone unnoticed either by local or international communities.

The introduction of new interactive digital media to the Arab societies has unleashed energy, creativity, and bottled up ideas that simply did not have an outlet before. The diversity of views, extraordinary discourse and exchange of information represented in this medium is unprecedented. Algerians can discuss Berber nationalism, Egyptian women can campaign to fight corruption, and the Sudanese can raise awareness of their plight in Darfour. Politicized messages promote changes such as in the case of Lebanon's Cedar revolution and the Egyptian secularists. These are voices that were not heard before (urls available as endnote). This type of activity may be viewed as a catalyst for democracy. There is much belief that Citizen Journalism has impacted mainstream media, irked governments and helped Arabs gain higher levels of freedom, yet some scholars insist that there is little evidence that it has made the region more democratic. (Best & Wade, 2005) Many critics also believe that because internet use and access are not very high, then these messages are not necessarily reaching a critical mass.

According the United Nations Millennium Development Goals Report the average number of internet connections in the Arab countries is way below the world average. Less than 10% of the population uses the internet. Yet, access and use are growing at a fast pace. However, citizen journalism has impacted traditional media too. Here, the critics' argument would be weak as traditional media particularly television enjoys a high penetration amongst the Arab peoples. Therefore, those who have never seen a Facebook account can still receive a powerful group message when its messages are replayed on national television. The following section looks at the impact that these technology-enabled citizens have had on traditional media as a first stop analysis of the concept of an emergent democracy.

Citizen Journalism Impacts the Traditional Media

Despite variances between different countries in the Arab Region, by and large most print and broadcast media have long been controlled. This static control resulted in much out dated content being presented to Arab audiences for several decades until the arrival of satellite television. Satellite television revolutionized media in the region, allowing for alternate opinions and thoughts. However, that was not the only venue for such variation. Suppressed views also began to appear with the introduction of another new medium, the Internet. With opposition websites and censored newspaper articles appearing online, it became clear that citizens instinctively knew how to harness the power of the Internet.

(Sreberny, 2001). Later, as the newer internet blogging technology platform became popular world-wide, Arabs too enlisted as members of the blogosphere. Convention has it that Salam Pax the Iraqi architect who blogged from Baghdad during the 2004 war was the First Arab to blog (Hamdy & Mobarak, 2004), but he was not alone for long. More and more bloggers came on board adopting this platform to express their opinions on topics that that rarely had been approached publicly. With English content that reflected mostly the views and psyche of the westernized elites, Sand Monkey, Baheyya, Riverbend, Sabah's Blog, The Black Irish Blog, the Arabist and Ghalia's Cocktail Blog grabbed the attention of their readers. (Lynch, 2007) These early bloggers addressed sensitive political issues, human rights abuses and other societal problems. They also discovered the power of their writings. They found that their blogs could provide freer information, compete with newspapers and television, become a tool for mobilization and attract like-minded citizens, and frequently attract international attention to their plights. (Levinson, 2005) It is hard to pin point exactly what happened next, but it is safe to say that soon afterwards a large number of bloggers began to blog in their native Arabic language, expanding the blogger base, the reader base, and the impact. New enabled voices began to blog furiously across the blogosphere. The most notable of these early successful online activism stories has been that of the Kefaya movement. An Egyptian opposition movement that included a variety of opposition parties and had a strong online component to its organization. Using mailing lists, emails, discussion groups, and more importantly blogging - their protests had an initial success. Individual bloggers gained fame through this movement, some like Alaa Abdel Fatah gained time in prison. (Zuckerman, 2006) Other notable citizen journalists include Wael Abbas the author of the Egyptian Awareness Blog, who not only blogged during the Kefaya movement but raised awareness of the frequency of police brutality, when he posted a video depicting police violence, and later scooped a story on female harassment in Cairo. (Mansour, 2007) Bahrain's blog and moblog 2005 directed protests (Schleusener,

2007), and Lebanon's extensive debate following Hariri's assassination and the ensuing Mehlis report are also representative of these notable blogging moments. (Hamdy, Alternative Arab Voices: A Depiction of the Usage of Blogs in Cyberspace, 2006) Encouraged by earlier bloggers and their ability to be heard many more bloggers joined their ranks. Today it is estimated that there are more than 40, 000 Arabic blogs, in relation to internet penetration in the region this number is substantial. (Implacable Adversaries: Arab Governments and the Internet, 2006) As Internet use grows in the Arab region and as a wider range of voices are heard on the Internet, cyber-activists are potentially positioned to become more influential. Certainly, the majority of the blogs may not contain significant content, but some of these bloggers have created an elite force that has been empowered by technology and is creating an impact on their readers, ordinary citizens and the traditional media. Traditional Arab media cannot eternally maintain its hegemony; citizen journalism is challenging their control over audiences. Alternative media is not only attracting readers but have directly changed the mainstream media's agenda. Media scholar Marc Lynch 2007 has observed the influence of these acts of citizen journalism. Dividing Arab bloggers into three categories of activists, bridge-bloggers, and public-sphere bloggers he has noted their heightened power during political peaks that affect the region.

With their no-holds-barred approach these bloggers have challenged Arab media, which have more than often than not steered clear of the mention of contentious issues. There have been several well documented cases where bloggers forced media to bring these issues to their agenda and other cases where the media were inspired by their efforts. Arab media could no longer ignore internet activities as they began to incorporate citizen journalism tips and notes in their coverage, chase the same stories, interview bloggers, and Facebook activists, invite them to their talk shows, and often openly approve of their candor. A legendary case in point is that of the bloggers who exposed the sexual harassment incident that took place during a public holiday in downtown Cairo in 2006.

Mainstream state media chose to ignore the issue for several days. However, when the Associated Press and satellite television channels picked up the story from blog entries, the case eventually hit media with considerable power. No longer was the story a report of an incident but a topic for public debate, and mainstream media became a forum for discussing the plight of women in a country where sexual harassment is a commonly practiced social ill. (Tahawy, 2006) Another noteworthy documentation is that of the Muslim Brotherhood Internet experience in Egypt. Following the ban of their official website in 2004 they learned how to decentralize their message by moving their presence to eighteen sites promoting their individual political candidates. Encouraged by the Kefaya movement's use of cyber activism the outlawed opposition group has taken to online communication furiously, with tens of individual bloggers partaking in the blogging of personal narratives of the Mubarak government's abuse of their members and challenging their brotherhood elders with their tech savvy approach to dissidence. These compelling stories often made their way into traditional media. (Ajemian, 2008).

In another incident, that of Egypt's April 6 "Facebook movement", a direct impact on mainstream media has been recorded. As the disaffected citizen journalists move on to newer technologies such as the popular social networking Facebook, Egypt has witnessed a group of citizens mobilize 80,000 supporters to protest the rise in food prices of 2008. The Facebook group broadened support for a textile workers' protest and simultaneously became a topic of coverage for mainstream media. Both state-owned and independent media gave considerable mention to the lobbying of the Facebook group, not to mention the increased coverage following the arrest of the young woman, Israa Abdel Fatah, the group creator. (Masloski, 2008). In addition, evidence also shows that prior to the first Facebook girl arrest, that as soon as Facebook use became popular in Egypt many lively groups appeared instantly. During Ramadan of 2008 one of the most popularly viewed television dramas on Arab satellite television was that of "King

Farouk". The popularity of this drama generated a series of royalist Facebook groups that carried pictures, information and even letters from members of Egypt's former monarchy. YouTube was also quickly populated by Royal family memorabilia, interviews, and other such curios. Young people paid attention. The unusualness of this occurrence caused for several highly viewed talk shows to refer to these groups and YouTube postings. Creators of the groups were invited to the shows and print media wrote about them. Another remarkable example of the influence of citizen journalism came about in Kuwait. In January of 2006 when the death of the Emir increased audience traffic on the internet, bloggers took advantage of the situation and lobbied for a reduction in the number of electoral districts prior to the parliamentary elections. The "Orange Movement" campaign was successful in part because voters could read blog entries in daily newspapers, amplifying their impact.(Lynch, 2007) Nevertheless, these are not the only cases of direct measurable impact on the media, there have been many. One of the more unusual influences has been the case of the Israel-Hizbollah conflict of 2006 where a marriage of alternative and traditional mediums was noted. An unusual blend of cross media platforms were used to cover this war extensively by Internet bloggers and traditional media, with both types of communicators covering and analyzing each others output.

New Alternative Media

Traditional journalists posted shocking war images on their personal blogs, whilst bloggers analyzed and commented on the media. Some mainstream media took this marriage a step further by hiring citizen journalists to blog for their media outlet. A sizeable amount of the information flow was contributed via new technologies. Bloggers, YouTubers and others both in and out of Lebanon and hand in hand with newspaper reporters, radio commentators and television journalists ferociously added to the story. (Ward, 2007).

Research and commentary and analysis on this impact are abundant in the literature on the changes that have taken place on the Arab media landscape. In actual fact, citizen journalists also credit themselves with what they perceive as their powerful impact on traditional media. They believe that they have emerged as strong alternative media as they do not have the same political agenda that the mainstream media have. They also cite the use of citizen journalism news reports, video clips, and pictures by traditional journalists, and the cooperation between citizen journalists and mainstream journalists as evidence that they had actually raised the ceiling on press freedoms while influencing traditional media. (Zekri, 2008). Nonetheless, it is difficult to find mainstream media professionals willing to acknowledge the existence of this situation. During an interview, veteran publisher Hisham Kassem did not acknowledge that citizen journalism in the Arab region had such a strong influence. Because of limited resources that these citizens have, they could not in his opinion replace traditional media. Blogger's most important role has been that of "watchdog of the watchdog" often causing media to be more accountable for their work. Citizen journalists can be the Arab world's fifth estate, monitoring its stale and unethical fourth estate.

Emphasizing that their influence is particularly strong on the new independent media, Kassem views these activated citizens as an army of alert observers who publish their comments, post their reactions, criticisms, and analysis instantly. (Personal Communication, February, 28, 2008) This role is one which citizen journalists such as Jordanian blogger Naeem Tarawnah also acknowledge. Tarawnah asserts that bloggers can stand afar and comment instantly on media by expressing their views on every worked printed or broadcasted in the Arab or foreign press on the region. (Tarawnah, 2008) Kassem further admits that, even though citizen journalists could not replace mainstream media reporting, they have, however, on several occasion acted as foot soldiers for Arab journalists by going out and fighting on the field first, pushing the envelope and achieving more press freedom. His comment indicates that, despite his reluctance to admit the challenge, there has been a power shift. It bears mentioning that whether local media acknowledge this impact or not, there is strong evidence that Arab citizen journalists have certainly grabbed the attention of western media.

It is hard to think of a single prestigious publication or broadcast station that has not covered the efforts of the rising activism performed by Arabs using the Internet and other digital technologies. From The Financial Times to the Washington Post from CNN to the BBC the highlight has been on the democratizing effects of blogs, YouTube, Yahoo groups and Facebook vis-à-vis the Arab region. Immortalized for their calls for political, economic and social reforms this elite group of communicators have learned to court the western press. Even those voices who were initially marginalized for their conservative political views, such as the Muslim Brotherhood bloggers, eventually gained their share of the spotlight. (Ajemian, 2008) There is also considerable evidence that it is possible to link to Arab blogs through the pages of prestigious newspapers and other international media online. In that sense a reader of the LA Times is more likely to receive information from an Arab blogger than to ever read an article in the *Sharq Al Awsat* or *Ahram* newspaper. These bloggers also have an equal chance of impacting individual western journalists who are also reading and observing these blogs. (Lynch, 2007). If it were not for this precise impact on traditional media, cyberspace may have remained a safe and exclusive domain for a few influential opinion leaders to discuss the issues that concern them. It was probably when these internet deliberations moved so quickly to a wider public that governments began to respond.

Authorities Confronted and Media Laws Challenged

In most countries in the Arab regions, governments have promoted the Internet and other digital technologies. They are perceived as a symbol of modernity and sophistication and as a development mechanism that must be supported as it would attract foreign investment and could ultimately cause for a leap into the information society. They have aggressively encouraged the adoption of new information and communication technologies. Indeed these new information highways have on the whole not been hindered by Arab governments. To the extent that newly created democratic spaces were not challenged, citizens enjoyed unprecedented flows of information unbothered by the authorities, that is, until the authorities noticed that all this freedom could lead to unintended consequences.

Cyber-activists have since been arrested, detained, harassed, pressured, assaulted, and even sentenced across the region. Adopting crude methods of intimidation several Arab governments have used draconian measures to control the digital voices of dissent. Egypt, Syria, Tunisia, Bahrain, and Saudi Arabia have all been guilty of such offenses. In Egypt, Alaa Abdel Fatah author of the award wining "Alaa and Manal's bit bucket" blog was detained by authorities following his involvement with the Kefaya movement online. (Reporters without Borders, 2006) Karim Abdel Amer is still in prison following his four year sentence for his atheist postings and insults to President Mubarak. Abdel Moneim Mahmoud, the Muslim Brotherhood blogger was arrested but not charged. (Blogger Abdul Moneim Freed, But Kareem Amer Still Held, 2007) Wael Abbass charges that the government of Egypt pressured YouTube administrators into dropping his video posts (Anderson, 2007) and Saudi Arabian blogger Fouad Ahmed Al-Farhan was released after four months in prison with no charge. (Ambah, 2008) Morocco's Fouad Mourtada was accused of usurping the identity of a member of the royal family on Facebook. (Williams, 2008) Although he was later pardoned, the accusation is one more example of an Arab government's over reaction to the democratic space. Tunisian courts have sentenced Slim Boukhdir for his blogging (Critical writer jailed in Tunisia, 2007) and the UAE has censored controversial blog content. (Weblogs soar in Gulf states , 2006) The list is long and continues to be updated. Others have not been arrested or harassed but have had their sites sabotaged, rendering them ineffective. Saudi Eve and other women in Saudi Arabia have been blocked as a consequence of the wrath of the conservative bloggers who search the internet scouring for unsuitable female expression and reporting them to government censors. (Abou-Alsamh, 2006) Similarly, Coptic blogger Hela Botros was obliged to close down her blog due to Egypt police pressure, but this pressure was before the Council of State Administrative Court ruled that authorities can block or suspend any site that threatens Egypt's "national security".

No need to pressure, now it is legal to shut down the root of the problem to the government. (Reporters Without Borders, 2006) Governments from Morocco to Syria to Oman are struggling with ways to minimize the damage caused by Twitters, Blogs, YouTube, Second Life, Text messaging, Flicker, Facebook, Podcasts and so on. Governments are becoming more aware that this activism is only the first generation of virtual civil society gatherings and activities. Social networking has already gained ground in the Middle East, and cell phone usage is booming; producing millions of members (Shannon, 2008) and facilitating more of the dreaded cyber-activism.

As previously mentioned, for decades these governments had become accustomed to controlling the flow of information through state-owned or state approved media. With the introduction of satellite television and the Internet, the Arab world has slowly changed and governments have reluctantly accepted alternative views and controversial opinions albeit in crab like steps, in a forward backward forward motion. (Media Sustainability Index (MSI) –Middle East & North Africa (MENA), 2005) In this context, it can be said that governments have, despite the added headache that comes with these new technologies, accepted what they bring. However this may simply be because of the lack of legislation to regulate these novel environments.

Laws and Emerging Social Media

In the absence of laws that address digital content there is a huge gap in terms of content regulation. The majority of countries in the region have instituted laws that address the technical aspects of the digital era. In rare instances is there any mention of content or issues related to freedom of speech in these new laws. Furthermore, digital writers are not treated as journalists or broadcast professionals, thus press laws cannot be used to protect them. It is for this reason that when there has been prosecution of content authors, penal codes have been used. Media outlets are transiting; the old methods by which media functioned are changing profoundly. The laws that were used to govern the old forms of media are no longer valid. Recently the Arab governments have responded to that dilemma by ratifying the Arab Charter for Satellite Television. Although strongly criticized by opponents ("Arab Media: How Governments Handle the News", 2008) it has been embraced by officials, some media scholars, and various professionals. (Allam, 2008).

Similarly the debate on Internet governance has also taken root. During the 2006 Tunis Convention of the Arab Interior Ministers Council, a call on Arab countries to unite their effort to ward off terrorism and to enact legislation that would allow them to fight communication that promotes extremism was made. (Implacable Adversaries: Arab Governments and the Internet) If such legislation is adopted, higher control will be given to government arms with regards to online communication. This act could undermine the efforts of Arab citizen journalism. Yet, regional regulation would not work for a global medium. Furthermore with the variance in cultural habits, traditions and customs among countries of the region, it would be difficult to find a common ground. For instance, in the case of Saudi Arabia which is a very conservative society, it was the actual citizens who sent in hundreds of suggestions a day on what sites the government should block. (Walton, 2007) In other countries such as Egypt the Internet has no access limitations to date. However, the government is currently drafting new audiovisual laws that if passed, would propose severe punishment to those who deviate from the norms through the transmission of offensive material on any digital platform. (El Sayed, 2008) In essence, reactions to digital content have differed from one country to another. Reactions have ranged from those who use filters to block undesirable sexual, religious, and culture content such as the UAE to those who like Egypt are mostly concerned with political incitement.

Despite fears expressed by proponents of Internet freedoms that there is a regional regulation framework currently underway, this outcome is not yet the case. Nonetheless, the future may see a push toward a regional regulator particularly with an increase in threats to the ruling regimes from Islamic groups. (Personal Communication Media Scholar and author of Satellite Charter Dr. Hussein Amin June 16, 2008). Perhaps Arabs have no plans to collaboratively regulate the digital highways; however, earlier during the World Summit on Information Society (WSIS 2005) a dialogue between world governments and the Internet community began, indicating that a global process could be underway. The signs show that there is an emerging conceptual framework that will involve governments from around the world, the private sector, civil society and the Internet community to be used for global governance of the medium. (Kummer, 2007) Sure there are apprehensions that range from limitations on freedom of expression and human rights to an unbalance in the relationship between governments and civil society, but inevitably this initiative has the potential also to lead to the tackling of global issues of concern.

Regional Democratization and Global Dimensions

Having said all this, the question emerges as to whether the Internet and related technologies so readily adopted by Arab Citizen Journalists has had an effect on democratizing the region. Sure, the region has seen an exponential growth in amount of information and its flow. It is also true that there is an intense expansion in communicative spaces and ideological variety. Furthermore,

more communication is occurring among citizens, which are also of vital importance to theories of democracy. However, these facts are still not guarantees that ICT empowerment will lead to democracy.

The region has witnessed embryonic movements gain small success, such as the case of Kefaya and the case of Kuwait bloggers or the April 6 Facebook strike, but it is important too to keep a balanced perspective and not to exaggerate the impact of these events. It is also important to accept that the Arab citizen's consciousness-values beliefs and moral reasoning must support the democratic idea before a democracy evolves. No amount of text messaging, YouTubing or Wikipeding can bypass that consent. The ethics of democracy rotate around the notion that people can make rational decisions to govern themselves. The Arab people have not reached this consensus. The internet may have increased the space for discourse, exchange of ideas, and engagement, but the reality is that if the Arab world is becoming more democratic, then it is doing so at a painfully slow rate. To date with little exception there is not a single government that can be described as truly democratically elected. Yes social action can be enhanced by technologies, but it cannot force an active involvement of citizenry. Moreover, as Ito (2003) warns, new technologies can also empower terrorists or totalitarian regimes. Terrorists, jihadis and other radicals have proved to have been empowered by these technologies. So too can authoritarian rulers be empowered. Undoubtedly these technologies can either enhance or deteriorate democracy. In the Arab context the verdict has not yet been made.

Conclusion and Summary

Citizens of the Arab world have harnessed new technologies ranging from online news sites, blogs, vblogs, YouTube, podcasts to SMS text messages, mobile phone web publishing, and facebook groups to produce and disseminate their journalism and advocacy faster than government can control, regulate or censor. Similar to their western counterparts, citizen journalism enthusiasts fueled by the new communication revolution, both technologically and philosophically have chipped into government media hegemony and private media powers, causing a deeply seated fear of citizen journalist empowerment. Taking advantage of a plethora of these innovative technologies and open source tools to become reporters and activists, many Arabs, both intentionally and unintentionally, have provided significant reports, analysis, and commentaries as well as mobilization for causes when mainstream media has been absent. Often the product of citizen journalists has had powerful implications, sometimes of national importance, not only confronting mainstream media and authorities for their deficiencies, but also challenging existing press laws and legal boundaries.

The chapter also has investigated various examples of citizen journalism including the highlighting of incidents of sexual harassment in Egypt, promotion of Berber nationalism in North Africa, the politicized messages promoting Lebanon's Cedar revolution, the mobilization of people by the Kefaya movement in Egypt, the dissent of the younger members of the Muslim Brotherhood via new technologies, monitoring of feminists actions in Saudi Arabia, the liberals who advocate for more personal freedoms, the Arab socialism revivalists via e-groups, the two females, Arab Christian thinkers, the atheists, the critics of the Bahraini rulers, the Darfur video bloggers, and the formation of royalists facebook groups in Egypt. As people have become more engaged in citizen media and have become more involved in transforming the way information is gathered and is disseminated, they have served not only to create more information and to shift the balance of power away from traditional sources, but they are also giving the opportunity for those voices that had never been heard and those voices that have converged in opposition to oppression in the Arab world to be heard outside of their confinements. This citizen activism has triggered an often fierce reaction by security apparatuses in the region. Furthermore, this citizen journalism has discussed and analyzed the current laws and methods used to govern those nationals who do choose to join the growing number of global citizen journalists.

References and Notes

Arab Media: How Governments Handle the News". (2008, February 8).
    Retrieved March 4, 2008, from The Economist:
    http://www.economist.com/world/africa/displaystory.cfm?story_id=10666436.Abou-
    Alsamh, R. (2006, June 19). Saudi women unveil opinions online. Retrieved June 24,
    2008, from The Christian Science Monitor:
    http://www.csmonitor.com/2006/0619/p06s02- wome.html

Ajemian, P. (2008, January 28). The Islamist opposition online in Egypt and Jordan. Retrieved
    June   14,   2008,   from   Arab   Media   &   Society:
    http://www.arabmediasociety.com/?article=577

Allam, R. (2008, February 19). "Satellite TV Content Regulation: One Step Forward".Retrieved
    March   4,   2008,   from   Daily   News   Egypt:
    http://www.dailystaregypt.com/article.aspx?ArticleID=11970

Ambah, F. S. (2008, April 27). Saudi Activist Blogger Freed After 4 Months in
    Jail Without Charge. Retrieved June 14, 2008, from Washingtonpost.com:
    http://www.washingtonpost.com/wpdyn/content/article/2008/04/26/AR2008042601470.h
    tml

Anderson, K. (2007, November 28). YouTube suspends Egyptian blog activist's account.
    Retrieved June 14, 2008, from *News Blog:*
    http://blogs.guardian.co.uk/news/2007/11/youtube_suspends_egyptian_blog.html

Annabelle, S. (2001). Mediated Culture in the Middle East: Diffusion, Democracy, Difficulties.
    Gazette Vol. 63(2-3) , 101- 119.

Barber, B. (1984). Strong Democracy: Participation Politics for the New Age. Berkeley:
    University of California Press.

Barlow, J. P. (1996, February 8). A Declaration of the Independence of Cyberspace Retrieved
    June 10, 10, fromhttp://homes.eff.org/~barlow/Declaration-Final.html

Bell, D. (1973). The Coming of the Post Industrial Society. New York: Basic .

Berman, J., & Daniel, W. J. (1997). Technology and Democracy. Social Research, Vol. 64, No 3
    Fall , 1313-1319.

Best, M. L., & Wade, K. W. (2005, October). The Internet and Democracy: Global Catalyst or
    Democratic Dud? Retrieved June 10, 2008, from http://ssrn.com/abstract=870080

Blogger Abdul Moneim Freed, But Kareem Amer Still Held. (2007, June 4). Retrieved June 14,
    2008, from *Reporters Without Borders:* http://www.rsf.org/article.php3?id_article=21995

Castells, M. (2008). The New Public Sphere: Global Civil Society,
    Communication Networks, and Global Governance. The ANNALS of the American
    Academy of Political and Social Science, 78-93.

Critical writer jailed in Tunisia. (2007, November 27). Retrieved June 14, 2008, From Committee
    to Protect Journalists CPJ News
    Alert:http://www.cpj.org/news/2007/mideast/tunisia26novt07na.html

El Sayed, M. (2008, July 17-23). Airwaves. Retrieved July 29, 2008, from Al Ahram .Weekly
    Online: http://weekly.ahram.org.eg/2008/906/eg6.htm

El-Nawawy, M., & Iskandar, A. (2002). AL-JAZEERA: How the Free Arab
    News Network Scooped the World and Changed the Middle East. Westview Press.

Fam, M. (2008, May 5). Egyptian Political Dissent Unites Through
    Facebook:Activists Make Use of New Technology Across Arab World. Retrieved June 9,
    2008, from The Wall Street Journal:
    http://online.wsj.com/article/SB120975285862963213.html

Gilder, G. (1992). Life after television: The coming transformation of television and the American
    Life. New York: W.W. Norton & Company.

Hamdy, N. (2006). Alternative Arab Voices: A Depiction of the Usage of Blogs in Cyberspace. International Association for Media and Communication Research IAMCR. Cairo, Egypt.

Hamdy, N., & Mobarak, R. (2004). Iraq War Ushers in Web-Based Era. In R. Berenger, Global Media Go to War: Role of News and Entertainment Media During the 2003 Iraq War (pp. 245-254). Spokane: Marquette Books.

Implacable Adversaries: Arab Governments and the Internet. (n.d.). Retrieved June 15, 2008, from The Arab Network for Human Rights Information: http://www.openarab.net/en/node/346

Implacable Adversaries: Arab Governments and the Internet. (2006). Retrieved March 2, 2008, from The Arabic Network for Human Rights Information (HRinfo): http://www.openarab.net/en/reports/net2006/blogger.shtml

Ito, J. (2003). Emergent Democracy. Retrieved June 12, 2008, from http://joi.ito.com/joiwiki/EmergentDemocracyPaper

Kummer, M. (2007). The debate on Internet governance: From Geneva to Tunis and Beyond. Information Polity 12 , 5-13.

Levinson, C. (2005, August 29). The Christian Science Monitor: Egypt's Online Voices of Dissent. Retrieved April 20, 2008, from AlterNet: http://www.alternet.org/story/24525/

Lips, M., & Jaap, B. (2005). Who Regulates and Manages the Internet Infrastructure? Democratic and Legal Risks in Shadow Global Governance. Information Polity 10 , 117-128.

Lynch, M. (2007). Blogging the New Arab Republic. Retrieved June 12, 2008, from Arab Media& Society: http://www.arabmediasociety.com/topics/index.php?t_article=32

Mansour, M. (2007, November 3). Is blogging a bursting bubble? Retrieved June 12, 2008, from Daily News Egypt: http://www.dailystaregypt.com/article.aspx?ArticleID=10091

Masloski, A. (2008, May 8). Fiction meets reality in Egypt. Retrieved June 14, 2008, from Middle East Times: http://www.metimes.com/Opinion/2008/05/08/fiction meets reality_in_egypt/2658/

Media Sustainability Index (MSI) – Middle East & North Africa (MENA). (2005). Retrieved June 15, 2008, from IREX: http://www.irex.org/programs/MSI_MENA/2005/MSIMENA05_summary.asp

Reporters Without Borders. (2006, June 22). Retrieved June 14, 2008, from Police Free Award-Winning BloggerAlaa Abd Al Fattah: http://www.rsf.org/article.php3?id_article=17660

Reporters Without Borders. (2006, November 7). Retrieved June 24, 2008, from List of the 13 Internet enemies: http://www.rsf.org/article.php3?id_article=19603

Rheingold, H. (1992/2000). Virtual communities: Homesteading on the electronic frontier . Cambridge: MA: MIT Press.

Sakr, N. (2001). Satellite Realms: Transnational Television, Globalization and the Middle East. London: I.B. Taurus.

Schiller, H. (1996). Information inequality . New York: Routledge.

Schleusener, L. (2007, February). From Blog to street: The Bahraini public sphere in transition . Retrieved June 14, 2008, from Arab Media & Society: http://www.arabmediasociety.com/countries/index.php?c_article=34

Shannon, V. (2008, March 6). Social Networking Moves to the Cellphone. The New York Times , p. p.7. Sparks, C. (2005).

Sparks, C. (2005). Media and Global Public Sphere: An Evaluative Approach. In W. D. Yong, M. Shaw, & S. Neil, Global Activism Global Media (pp. 34-49). London. Ann Arbor: Pluto Press.

Sun, S. L., & Barnett, G. A. (1999). The International Telephone Network and Democratization. Journal of the American Society for Information Science , 45(6), 411-421.

Tahawy, M. A. (2006, November 16). Blogs and women force sexual harassment onto Egypt's agenda. Retrieved March 4, 2008, from

http://www.saudidebate.com/index.php?option=com_content&task=view&id=432&Itemi
d=166

Tarawnah, N. (2008). Presentation "Case Study: The Black Iris Blog". United
Nations University- International Leadership Insitute. Aman Jordan March
15 .

Toffler, A. (1980). The Third Wave. New York: Morrow.

UAE most wired country in Arab world. (2008, June 2). Retrieved June 10, 2008,
From Gulfnews.com:
http://archive.gulfnews.com/technology/developments/10218075.html

Walton, D. C. (2007). Is Modern Information Technology Enabling the Evolution of a More
Direct Democracy. World Futures , 63:365-385.

Ward, W. (2007, February). Uneasy Bedfellows: Bloggers and mainstream media report the
Lebanon conflict. Retrieved June 14, 2008, from Arab Media & Society:
http://www.arabmediasociety.com/topics/index.php?t_article=52

Weblogs soar in Gulf states . (2006, June 26). Retrieved June 14, 2008, from Al
Jazeera English Website:
http://english.aljazeera.net/English/archive/archive?ArchiveId=23619

Williams, C. (2008, February 25). Morocco jails Facebook faker. Retrieved June 14, 2008, from
The Register:
http://www.theregister.co.uk/2008/02/25/morocco_prince_facebook_sentence/

Zekri, M. (2008). Steps on the Road. Mutual Support Between the Internet and Human Rights.
Cairo: The Arab Network For Human Rights Information

Zuckerman, E. (2006, September 16). Alaa on Egyptian Blogs and Activism. Retrieved June 12,
2008, from My heart's in Accra: http://www.ethanzuckerman.com/blog/2006/09/16/alaa-
onegyptian- blogs-and-activism/

Chapter Five

The Issues Educators Face in the Convergence Global Marketplace

Anthony Esposito
Edinboro University of Pennsylvania

Media convergence is the most significant development in the news industry in the last century. The ability to interchange text, audio, and visual communication over the Internet has fundamentally transformed the way news organizations operate (Criado & Krapelin, 2003). It is not uncommon for the field of mass communication to change.

However, throughout the history of journalism, it has been common for journalists to study one medium, such as traditional print or broadcast, and to anticipate a career working only in their chosen field. This commonplace has inherently changed, as the 21st century journalist and communication practitioner should be able to write and deliver news content in a variety of formats. As a matter of fact, it seems nearly impossible to follow developments in technology, business, or journalism without encountering the word convergence.

How does convergence change what is being taught in various communication and media programs throughout the country? Will these changes enhance or detract from the specialized education students receive from their respective professors? Data reveals that more than eight out of ten educators and eight out of ten news directors practice/teach convergence in some manner (Tanner & Duhe, 2005). Nevertheless, it must be noted that some educators and academic programs have an aversion towards convergence because the student does not receive training in a specialized area of study. This important debate lingers on, but it is this debate that needs to be addressed by both institutions of higher learning that focus on media and the organizations that will be hiring people in print and broadcasting in the near future.

This chapter looks at three issues: First, how is convergence being implemented in various forms of the communication, speech, broadcasting, and media programs around the country? To achieve this purpose, a broad definition to the term convergence is provided to the reader. Entailed in this chapter is a brief history of the term and how it has been implemented in the discipline of media and communication.

Second, for educational purpose, I have looked at how the term convergence was employed in a setting like a classroom in a college or a university. Third, I have provided an argument on the strength and weakness of this development and highlight its theoretical implications for the twenty-first century and teaching environment, be it a classroom or training session or a workshop. It is argued that various institutions and organizations, with regard to convergence, would either follow or discard these templates. In addition, this chapter concludes with suggestions and recommendation for future communication practitioners on whether this practice should be embraced or castigated as our discipline moves towards our prospects for the upcoming decades.

Historical Background

Media convergence is a term that is defined from numerous perspectives by both people in the media and scholars interested in its impact upon media studies. Convergence generally means that all component platforms available for delivery to a web based operating system contribute to the overall information product. It also implies that information sharing and enhancement take place along the way (Killebrew, 2002).

Another interesting definition is posed by Criadio and Krapelin (2003) when they state, "convergence journalism is defined as print, broadcast and online staffs forging partnerships in which journalists often work and distribute content across several news platforms" (p.3). These are just a few ways to define this term. However, these two definitions inform the reader of the power of this model. Audiences in the age of convergence can communicate in numerous areas. These include, but are not limited to, e-mail, online forums, and other interactive media that enable individuals more ease with those who create and publish mass communication content.

From operational perspectives, Media General's Tampa, Florida facility was one of the first to bring print, broadcast and online staffers under one roof dubbed the "News Center." As part of Media General's convergence efforts, journalists from the Tampa Tribune, WFLA-TV, and Tampa Bay Online came together to share news content (Colon, 2000). There are others, but I wanted to focus on the most seminal one for time purposes of this study.

Media convergence was not discussed in higher education or the media until the mid 1990s. However, others will espouse that this term has been in existence since the early 1980s. In fact, communication scholar Ithiel de Sola Pool in his seminal 1983 book, *The Technologies of Freedom,* described what he called the convergence of modes. Pool stated:

The explanation of the current convergence between historically separated modes of communication lies in the ability of digital electronics. Conversation, theater, news and text are all increasingly delivered electronically. Electronic technology is bringing all modes of communication into one grand system (p. 27).

This holistic model was not only established by academics, but also applied to the world of media organizations. Even before Pool's book was published, leading thinkers in journalism and academia were coming to realize that technological changes were going to affect the news media. William Paley, chairman of CBS, gave a speech to a broadcaster's convention in 1980, noting that, "the convergence of delivery mechanisms for news and information raises some critical First Amendment questions."

Moreover, one that embraced the term convergence was John Sculley, who became CEO of Apple Computers in 1983. Gordon asserts, "When the word convergence showed up in the business press in the 1980s and early 1990's, it was often in connection with Sculley and Apple" (p.11). The vision of the future seemed to increase in the 1990s, when the World Wide Web became mainstream and fulfilled the dreams and aspirations that Pool had predicted.

Moreover, Pool's vision was also established in the world of academia, especially in the area of modern media studies. In today's modern academic world, schools such as the University of Kansas and USC –Annenberg are fully committed to taking the multimedia approach to journalism education. Schools that established the early precinct, include the University of South Carolina, University of South Florida, and Brigham Young University. In fact, one of the first schools in the country to teach multimedia journalism was Brigham Young University. In 1995, the faculty there began talking about the best way to create "Super Reporters," reporters who would be able to move easily among print, broadcast, and online media (Wegner, 2005). The university became the cornerstone towards promoting media convergence in the classroom. In 1999, BYU started a three-year tradition of winning the Editor & Publisher award for the best online campus news site. Additionally, in 1997, The International Journal of Research into New Media addressed the creative, social, political and pedagogical issues raised by the advent of new media technologies (Tanner and Duhe, 2005).

Convergence in Media Organizations

Both media organizations and journalism educators appear to see convergence as important to the profession. Commencing in 2002 and finishing in 2003, Carrie Criado and Camille Krapelin, from Southern Methodist University, conducted a groundbreaking study to determine whether convergence journalism is taking hold in the United States media industries and university schools of journalism. Below are the key findings in their research endeavors. These include:

1. Both media organizations and journalism educators appear to see convergence as important to the future of the profession.

2. The vast majority of both newspapers and TV stations surveyed have forged convergence partnerships, defined as sharing of content and/or staff with another media platform - around nine in 10 newspapers and eight in 10 TV stations.

3. Likewise, university journalism programs have also moved toward convergence. Just under nine in 10 of the college administrators surveyed said they had incorporated, or begun to incorporate, cross-platform training into their coursework.

Convergence and Journalism Educators

The following sections will begin to answer the above questions with specificity and statistics. First, since media organizations do not have the time to train new graduates on media convergence, they expect these skills to be gleaned during an applicant's education. There appears to be a significant need for convergence training because of the demand for these skills. However, and most importantly, this training is not taking place on the job. Between journalism and television jobs, TV executives are more likely to prepare their journalists for convergence work. Bob Salesberg, RTNDA's chairman espouses the importance of this term to his profession when he asserts, "There is a reason convergence is a buzzword in the industry. Like streams emptying into a river, TV, radio, and print are all beginning to merge. We're not sure where the digital river will flow, but don't sit back while the waters rush past."

Journalism programs around the country feel that media convergence should be an important part of a student's education. 85 percent of the university programs included in the survey - both large and small, with many majors or few- have adapted their curriculum, or begun to adopt it, in response to the industry trend towards convergence (Criado and Krapelin, 2003). It should be noted that these programs are not truly converged, meaning that students work across platforms throughout their studies. Many who employ some form of convergence curricula said the changes represent a minor shift, meaning that is has been altered some to accommodate the industry emphasis on convergence.

Convergence in Newspapers and Television

Television managers find convergence to have some application when hiring a new candidate. 23.5% of TV managers find it important for a new hire. 49.0 said it would be somewhat important (Tanner and Duhe, 2005). It is not an essential skill. However, it is still one that is embraced by people in higher positions in various news agencies around the country. This is highlighted by Tanner and Duhe when they assert:

> *Without a doubt, convergence appears to be a growing trend among industry professionals, but with only 141 documented convergent relationships currently in the media industry, convergence still has a long way to go to saturate the industry.*

This is not an assertion of the secondary nature of this new paradigm, but maybe this practice is not as much a part of the modern day media as its success was predicted. It is calculated that only a few media companies are actually converged in the sense that they share news (Tomkins, 2001). But at times this research seems to misleading depending upon the source of the message. Even though it has been stated that convergent relationships are not saturating the market, it does seem that television executives still find it an important skill to possess for their employees. Current statistics infer that 88% of news directors said convergence was an important part of their institutional systems. In fact, just over eight in ten of the television stations surveyed are involved in some sort of convergence partnership, defined as the sharing of content and or staff with another media platform (Criado and Krapelin, 2003).

In addition, 83 percent of the TV stations involved in a convergence partnership involve a Web partner. For example, most stations provide some content to their Website partner. This usually consists of having reporters provide versions of stories they've written for a newscast to the Website. Nearly 75 percent of station managers surveyed said their staff members frequently contribute to the Web content in this way (Criado and Krapelin, 2003).

In comparison, newspaper managers, 16.9% felt convergence was very important, and 52.9% called it moderately important. Overall, 93 percent involved in a study said that some form of a convergence partnership was important. This partnership was with a Website. 62.3 percent of the relationships are with a site directly associated with the newspaper. However, in opposition, only 26 percent infer that their reporters write exclusive Web stories. It is true that Newspaper-Web partnerships are most common. But it should be noted that newspapers are also likely to be involved in a convergence partnership with a TV station. Nearly 70 percent of newspapers in convergence partnerships are associated with a TV station ((Criado and Krapelin, 2003).

In the above examples involving the convergence methods, both television stations and newspapers at least espouse the importance of convergence skills. I do find it interesting that instead of skills, it seems to be very important that convergence relationships exist. This does not mean it is not important. But not maybe as important as we are made to believe by both communication practitioners and academics in general.

Global Convergence in Higher Education

Journalism programs throughout the country seem to be moving towards implementing forms of convergence into their academic templates. It seems like more lip service is being given to the term in comparison to implementing these changes into the classroom. As illustrated earlier in this chapter, these changes have been minor. Since most of these programs represent fairly minor curriculum changes, few reflect a truly converged model. This is an important point. According to Craido and Krapelin (2003):

> *Most respondents (51.28 percent) described their programs as ones in which print, broadcast and other majors remain separate tracks of study, with no overlap. Nearly as many (46.15 percent) described a somewhat more converged model, saying that all journalism majors in their program are required to take classes in a range of mediums-such as writing for print, broadcast and online- but then specialize in one sequence. Only one respondent described his/her convergence program as "truly" converged, where students work across platforms throughout their studies (p 16).*

Some journalism/speech programs around the country usually offer separate tracks for their students. This is commonplace around the country. Another theme appears to be the training of students in a range of media, although the emphasis remains on print, with 89 percent of convergence programs training most or all of their students to write for print media. In addition, 46 percent also train most or all of their students to write for the Internet. This is a skill that all companies expect a recent graduate to possess at the time of their hiring.

The one skill that is embraced by both academia and media organizations is the ability of the individual to conduct research on the Internet. In fact, some 95 percent of the convergence programs included in the survey train most or all of their students to use the Internet in this way. Numerous programs around the country embrace convergence in the classroom.

But it must be noted, that Brigham Young University (BYU), one of the leaders in this field, now feels that too much emphasis has been placed on convergence. The hiring of Dr. Stephen Adams as Dean in 2000 changed the way convergence would be studied in the classroom at BYU. Adams felt that students knew an abundance of information about an abundance of things, but didn't know very much in depth (Gordon, 2003). This seems to be one of the critiques leveled against this approach. By 2001, the school started to realize that the convergence experiment wasn't working. It must be noted, this is the same school that won numerous awards just two years prior to this time period.

One of the complaints was that it took away necessary depth in core writing classes, especially ones focused on print journalism. According to Adams (2004),"The school still did not have a sense that its convergence efforts were making much of an impact." He said, "students have not been getting convergence jobs; they're getting jobs in traditional journalism venues." In the end, BYU decided to walk away from the multimedia approach

Adams's rhetoric is understandable. However, it must be stated that for some high level programs, convergence can produce the new journalists of the future. The journalism program must decide what it wants to do with the resources it has available. There are still plenty of jobs out there for print, TV and online specialists and a plethora of needs for schools to provide depth and expertise in a single media platform. It is still the job of the academy to train students in the necessary skills of researching, writing, and obtaining information for news and TV stories. Meyers (2004) provides his view on convergence in the classroom when he states, "But tackling convergence in the academic world is not without its own distinct challenge. Some believe the merger of jobs in converged newsrooms may either diminish the quality of the writing or the visuals" This is a concern also articulated by media organizations hiring recent college graduates in the field of media journalism. They feel that news writing and reporting skills are important for a new journalism hire. In addition, 100 percent across both academic and organizational groups found news judgment as an important criterion for future success in the profession. Also included were media law and ethics, and a broad liberal arts background (Tanner and Duhe, 2005). Certainly, these skills would be first gleaned by being in the classroom since most of the journalism programs around the country offer some series of convergence new writing classes. It would be a disservice to both students and employers for these skills not to be taught in the classroom.

Conclusion and Summary

Is convergence training preparing students for the media world of the twenty-first century? Is it needed? The answer to this question depends on the researcher conducting research in this area of study. As stated earlier, some students at BYU complained they worked hard to get into a good program but were forced to do many things they were not interested in doing (Tompkins, 2001). The student's rhetoric can be taken in numerous ways. First, they could be complaining like all college students that must take classes outside of their majors. Second, what they may be asserting can have some validity on the current job market. An eye opening statement that was gleaned by doing this research is that only 50 percent graduating with degrees are getting jobs in their fields. Yes convergence in the classroom is important. In fact, 72 % of educators believe that convergence is the future of mass communication (Campbell, 2003). In addition, the new media skills that are valued most highly by newspaper managers, journalism educators and TV executives would be the ability to research on the Internet. All three agreed that this would be important when making hiring decisions.

It seems that the gleaning of basic rudimentary skills seems to be of utmost importance to students graduating with degrees in media journalism and communication studies. Even though technology continues to play a role in how the modern day media person performs duties, the fundamentals of news writing and reporting remain of significant importance to industry leaders and media faculty. The basic skill of performing Internet research is a must for individuals pursuing jobs in respective media industries. Therefore, the job of providing these skills rests with the academy.

The journal of Chronicle of Higher education always brings this issue to light and confirms that further research needs to be conducted to address this area. Future academic research could explore the impact of journalism training and job hiring in the field of TV and newspaper journalism. Craido and Karpelin (2003) emphasized the importance of the topic of convergence and global communication to the academic community and the culture of media journalism. The authors argued:

Even with all the technological advancements that today's journalists enjoy, it may seem implausible and even detrimental to expect working journalists to excel in all areas of print, broadcast, and online writing.

Researchers throughout the world keep asking the same question: Would we end up with jacks-of-all trade or continue to have print, broadcast, and online specialists? Additional research is needed to determine the expectations of the twenty-first century Journalists. Perhaps, the best we can hope for at this juncture is to cultivate new writers who are rooted in the best traditions of journalism and who have a sense of how to present news and information with convergence in mind (p. 15).

References and Notes

Campbell, R. (2003). Media and Culture: An introduction to mass
communication. Boston: Bedford/St. Martin's Press.

Colon, A. (2000). The multimedia newsroom. Columbia Journal Review. 24-27.

Criado, C., & Krapelin, C. (2003). Convergence Journalism: Landmark U.S. media and
university study. Convergence Journlaim.com

De-Sola Pool, I. (1983). Technologies of Freedom. Cambridge, Mass: The Belknap
Press of Harvard University Press.

Gordon, R. (2006). Convergence defined. USC Annenberg: Online Journalism Review.

Killebrew, K. (November, 2002). Distributive and content model issue
Convergence: Defining aspects of mew media in journalisms venture.
Paper presented at the Dynamics of Convergent Media Conference.
Meyers, E. K. (2004). How journalism schools address the challenge of training online
journalists. www.newslink.org.

Tanner, A., & Duhe, S. (2005). Trends in mass education in the age of media Convergence:
Preparing students for careers in converging news environment. Studies in Media and
Information Literacy Education, 5, 3, 1-13.

Tompkins, A. I (2001). Convergence needs a leg to stand on. www.poynter.org/

Wenger Halpren, D. (2006). The road to convergence and back again.
www.bottomlinecom.com

Chapter Six

Television and Small-Nation Globalization

Bjorn Ingvoldstad
Bridgewater State University

When Mikhail Gorbachev initiated his policies of *glasnost* ("openness") and *perestroika* ("restructuring") soon after his rise to Soviet leadership in 1985, he did so to consolidate and reinvigorate socialism in the USSR and the Warsaw Pact. However unwittingly, though, these policies created an opportunity for far more than healthy discussion or waste reduction; rather than renew Soviet power, they were the means of its demise. *Glasnost* finally started to become more practice than theory in the wake of the Chernobyl disaster, and the government's public mishandling of crucial information. *Pererstroika* moved beyond restructuring of government organizations to the organization of governments, as Hungary and Poland both made moves towards gradual reforming the Communist Party out of power. Together, the combined force of *glasnost* and *perestroika* in socialist Europe created something of a "perfect storm" by 1989: Hungary opened its borders with the West, Polish round-table discussions quietly ushered Socialists out of power, the Berlin Wall fell, and Czechs shook their keys to welcome back Václav Havel and Alexander Dubček.

Seismic changes were taking place within the Soviet Union as well. On August 23rd, 1989, people from Estonia, Latvia, and Lithuania joined hands down the length of the Baltic republics to mark and mourn the 60th anniversary of the 1939 Molotov-von Ribbontrop pact, which sealed the fate of the Baltic in World War II.[i] Tentative earlier protests drawing public attention to Soviet annexation of the Baltic States on the eve of World War II conjoined with more widespread disenchantment with the way central leadership was dealing with their Western-most republics. Communist parties on the republic level began to break away from the center throughout the Baltic, and Lithuania went so far as to declare its re-independence from the Soviet Union on March 11, 1990, only months after the domino-like collapse of one Warsaw Pact government after another.

After an extended economic blockade by the Soviets, patience had worn thin with Moscow leadership. In January 1991, while the United States and its allies were fighting the First Gulf War, the USSR acted in a way it could not or dared not do during the 1989 Warsaw Pact dissolution: it fought back, or at least began to. Eerily reminiscent of earlier Soviet actions to quell popular unrest in Budapest (1956), Prague (1968), or Warsaw (1981), a hard-line decision was made to send OMON "Black Beret" troops (ostensibly to enforce Soviet red army conscription—the Soviets were in the midst of a decade-long war in Afghanistan) to the Lithuanian capital.[ii]

Independence leaders rightly feared the Soviets would re-assert their authority with force. Lithuanian Parliamentary Chairman Vytautas Landsbergis called on civilians—not just from Vilnius and the surrounding region, but from all over the country—to mobilize and surround key sites. Notably, beyond the parliament itself, the remaining sites were all media-related: the press house, the state radio and television studios, and the television tower. While the press house and broadcast studios saw skirmishes, it was at the television tower where the vast majority of casualties occurred. Fourteen unarmed civilians were killed on the grounds of the tower on the night of January 13th (see Saja, et. al, 1992).

In Šeduva (a small town of 3000 people where I performed my fieldwork a decade later) as throughout the country, townspeople were able to watch what was happing in Vilnius live on their television sets. The events of January 13 were broadcast on the state Lithuanian Television (LTV) until the OMON troops finally took the tower, briefly cutting transmission, and later announcing that "order" had been restored. Within a few days, armed troops rolled into Šeduva itself to secure the local television transmitter.[iii] Troops soon withdrew from town almost as fast as they had come. Within days, they were out of the country altogether and on to Latvia, where several more civilians were killed.[iv] Seemingly an improvised, stopgap measure, these shock troops soon retreated to the Soviet interior, ostensibly having proven their point. The independent government regained control of the airwaves. In seven months, the failed August coup in Moscow signalled the death knell for the Soviet Union; several months after that, on New Year's Eve, Gorbachev himself signed the declaration finally dissolving the USSR.

In January 1991, then, television had literally served as a site for a momentous political power struggle in Lithuania. As a result of Gorbachev's *glasnost* and *perestroika* reforms in the late 1980s, the Lithuanian SSR had greater control over what programming its citizens might be offered. When Lithuania stopped merely outpacing Moscow, and more emphatically attempted to break ties with central leadership in 1990, authorities chose to strike back with force. Thus, when the Lithuanian parliament called on its citizens to mobilize in non-violent defense of the nascent nation, they concentrated on defending key government buildings, including television production and broadcast facilities. Indeed, the OMON troops never raided the Lithuanian parliament building, as had been feared, but did indeed control television broadcasting for the duration of their occupation.

Television has also been a site of other, less deadly power struggles as well, particularly in terms of the operations of Lithuanian state television and its place within an increasingly neo-liberal domestic market. As throughout Europe, governments in Lithuania have struggled (and continue to struggle) with questions surrounding the efficacy, viability, and mandate of public broadcasting in the 21st century. In addition, several commercial networks now compete for the relatively lucrative advertising market within the country by offering a much wider range of programming than was ever available in the Soviet period.

As this brief history suggests, to study Lithuanian television is to study the political, economic, and social changes taking place within the country. If television—particularly satellite and cable television—constructs and fosters the "global village," how does this manifest itself in the villages around the globe? This chapter looks at television from three distinct, interconnected points of view in order to understand this global(izing). The investigation of these points of view happened on several levels; as the chapter proceeds, my notion of what counts as a "text" narrows, moving from broader industrial concerns to close reads of TV programming. Throughout the chapter, though, I return my discussion of television to the people I spoke to in Šeduva, foregrounding their local experience of TV viewing.

First, I will examine Lithuanian television as a delivery system, studying the ways cable and satellite technologies have (or have not) penetrated the everyday life of television viewership in Šeduva, in comparison with traditional terrestrial broadcasting. Next, I discuss the networks themselves, focusing on the three principal terrestrial networks within Lithuania. Further, this chapter discusses how service broadcasting has been forced to compete with commercial networks, and how national networks in turn have competed within a regional framework. Several programs produced by these Lithuanian networks can be roughly understood as "reality television," investigating in particular how this global programming phenomenon functions in a particular local/national market. The chapter concludes with a call for further research on the increasing penetration of cable and satellite delivery systems in Lithuania, as well on the role of television and digital convergence in the Lithuanian expatriate community.

Uneven Globalization: Cable, Satellite, and Terrestrial Broadcasting

Much discussion dealing with globalization and television centers on new delivery systems (e.g., cable and satellite) allowing a wider range of channels than ever before. In addition, the formatting of these systems, such as digital or high definition, offers further enhancements of these delivery systems. However, when the discussion shifts from utopian technological potentials to existing power structures, the mood becomes increasingly somber. Discussions of the political economy of this new era of television often focus on the ownership of delivery systems, networks, the one-way flow of programming from west to east, and so on.

Michael Curtin (1996) identifies the present moment as the "neo-network era," in which the traditional television network system has been supplanted by a complicated web of interconnectedness via several media platforms. While Curtin is certainly correct in identifying this shifting territory not only in the US but globally as well, it is also true that in certain territories the "network era" continues as well—or rather, that the "network" and "neo-network" frameworks exist simultaneously, in terms of both production and consumption. Audiences in metropolitan centers such as Vilnius can be understood as functioning within Curtin's "neo-network" mediascape. However, much of the rest of the country functions within a relatively more national, "network" mediascape in which Lithuania's national channels are not forced to compete with international programming via satellite or cable. Thus, the urban-rural gap, which points to broader sociological divisions in terms of class and upward mobility, is again re-inscribed in the ways in which television is consumed in the Lithuanian context.

Table 1 (next page) documents the rise in cable and satellite (Sat) penetration rates throughout Europe in the past decade.

**Table 1: Households receiving satellite and cable in Europe:
Selected countries, 1993 and 2003**

TV households receiving cable Households receiving cable

Country	(in millions), 2003	or sat. (%), 1993	or sat. (%), 2003
Lithuania	1.3	1.5	31.2
Latvia	0.8	0.7	53.8
Estonia	0.5	5.2	58.5
Czech Republic	3.9	20.5	29.5
Hungary	3.8	25.6	71.1
Poland	12.9	11.6	55.5
Germany	36.2	61.7	95.6
Netherlands	7.0	97.1	98.1
Norway	2.0	41.6	73.2
Sweden	4.0	58.8	67.2
Finland	2.1	40.9	44.1
Denmark	2.4	59.4	71.1
EUR12/25	176.1	29.6	55.5

(Sources: EAO *Statistical Yearbook 1994/1995*, p. 42; EAO *Statistical Yearbook 2004, Vol. 2*, p. 32)

[Note: European totals and averages are based on the twelve-nation European Community in 1993, and the then-pending twenty-five-nation European Union for 2003.]

One way to effectively understand Lithuania's "in-between-ness" in terms of television and globalization is to look at the levels of consumption of non-broadcast delivery systems on several different levels. Perhaps unexpectedly, variations in national penetration rates reveal an East-West divide. Less obvious and commonsensical is the fact that there are definite variations and divisions in both Western Europe and in the former Eastern Bloc. In addition, even within a given country, the penetration rates for these various delivery systems in *urban versus rural* areas is equally revealing. Not only that, it appears that the differences are shifting somewhat over time. In and of themselves, the results are not surprising—we should expect there to be a climb, even a significant climb, over a recent ten-year stretch. However, several notable items from this data present themselves. First, there is certainly an East-West divide: all told, Western nations have consistently higher penetration rates than Eastern ones. Lithuania's rate (1.5% in 1993, 31.2% in 2003) has remained well below the European average. Over time, this gap has shrunk significantly, and in some cases disappeared entirely. Indeed, in 2003 Poland's penetration rate (55.5%) equaled that of the EU, while Hungary and Estonia bettered it. On the other hand, Lithuania's situation has moved from a rate of only 5% of the EC in 1993 to over 56% of the EU in 2003.

Second, in addition to the shrinking gap between "East" and "West," we can see regional cleavages within both East and West that point to the relative inadequacy of these geo-political terms in the post-accession, twenty-five-nation European Union.

In 1993, the contrast in their situations was marked: the Central European economies not only had a two-year head start in terms of market reform compared to the Baltic States, they also had the advantage of not having to directly disentangle from the Soviet economy. Yet, by 2003, while Lithuania and the other Baltic nations (as well as Poland) have seen dramatic increases in penetration rates (500-1000%), Hungary (300%) has seen less of a change, explained by its relatively more mature market. Further, the Czech Republic has only seen a 50% increase over the decade—still substantial, yet nowhere near the levels elsewhere in the region, and nearly half the penetration rate of the EU average. In contrast, the Scandinavian countries have been a consistently strong market for cable and satellite, with Holland and Germany reaching nearly full penetration by the beginning of the 21st Century. If we understand satellite and cable usage to be a *means* as well as an *end* of globalizing forces, what these figures reveal is that, even within the European Union, there is unevenness in the way globalization is lived from country to country.

Finally, what this table fails to capture—and what I am still working to account for statistically—is the way in which cable and satellite are dispersed throughout urban and rural environments. This point is crucial to my project, because I believe it succinctly presents how the uneven nature of globalization can be seen not only from region to region, or even from nation to nation, but *within* this particular nation. Not only is this a function of urbanization in Lithuania, it is also a function of class. Satellite dishes have proliferated, for instance, on the roofs of Vilnius flats and the capital's suburban homes. However, outside of this political and economic hub, their absence is notable. The corollary, of course, is that urban income levels are significantly higher than that of rural areas—multi-channel both is a marker of affluence and a further cultural wedge between haves and have-nots.

In America, the actual cables for cable television are laid or even bundled with phone lines. In the past several decades, the USA has seen a methodical expansion of wired infrastructure redundant beyond urban centers not only to suburban areas but also to smaller towns. In Lithuania, the existing phone line network was much more tenuous. Not only was the quality of phone lines rather poor, phone penetration rates were less than optimal. Indeed, even for people who wanted to add a phone line (and anecdotally here I will mention that I knew several people who had waited *years* for a phone), it was not as easy as simply placing an order.

As I will discuss briefly in my concluding chapter, profound dissatisfaction with the existing land-telephone system was a major impetus for the explosion of cellular phone usage throughout the Baltic States.[v] In Lithuania, as in the EU accession states, cable and satellite penetration rates have lagged far behind the other fifteen member nations. Further, while my evidence on this point is anecdotal and observational, I would assert that this divide is not so much to be found in urban centers, but in rural areas. In other words, while I would guess that the penetration rates in Vilnius are not terribly lower than, say, Stockholm or Lisbon, the real difference is to be found in terms of *rural* penetration rates.

All of which points to the fact that discussing television and globalization in the context of the work in Šeduva presents interesting problems to theories of globalization. When academic discussion centers on the delivery of satellite and cable, the homogenizing effect of global channels, or the adaptation of global networks to local tastes (e.g., MTV India), it is difficult to sort out where the particular local situation of Šeduva might fit. Such small towns might fruitfully be understood as the structuring absence of globalizing industrial rhetoric. In this light, to consume cable or satellite is to link oneself with cosmopolitan life, with upward mobility, and with progress; conversely, to not have these multichannnel platforms is isolationist, rural, and culturally static (if not backward). However, rather than reify such industrial rhetoric, I want to problematize it by articulating a greater level of cultural complexity and negotiation than such rhetoric allows.

People have been signing up for cable in Šeduva—but slowly. One of the main selling points, apparently, has been more regular access to Russian networks. Russian programs had been translated on local broadcast stations through much of the 1990s, with licensing strategies subsequently shifting in Moscow to cable and satellite transmission. The sticking point for potential subscribers is the significant up-front costs of initial installation (several weeks' wages, on national average—though "average" salaries are hard to find in the small towns). Hence, a major drawback is the pricing scheme—the amount of money that subscribers must pay for the initial connection: hundreds of American dollars. Though the cost-per-month is much more reasonable, people must still pay for something that ostensibly was previously "free." While the subscription base bothers many, others question the re-importation of Russian programming. Indeed, there is something of a moral panic amongst cultural elites in Lithuania, which goes so far as to posit the so-called "Stockholm Syndrome" to explain the continued draw of Russian programming in the country.

Cable and satellite penetration levels have been much lower in rural, economically disadvantaged areas of the country than in the relatively flourishing urban centers. National television networks continue to play a major role in the Lithuanian mediascape—indeed, outside of major cities the "network" era never ended. However unevenly, though, the "neo-network" is indeed arriving in Lithuania, and perhaps one of the best places to observe its arrival is in the nation's hub of international trade and travel: its hotels.

In his foundational study *Television: Technology and Cultural Form* (2003), Raymond Williams writes of recognizing television's programming "flow" as part of a cross-cultural experience, a British citizen holed up in a Miami hotel due to a layover. A similar cross-cultural moment is now possible for anyone with a satellite dish without ever leaving home—provided you have a satellite dish at home. But nobody I worked with in Šeduva did: during the time of my fieldwork (2000-2002) cable television was nonexistent, and satellite usage was minimal. A teaching colleague in a nearby village had a dish, but nobody I knew in Šeduva itself had one that worked.[vi] Tellingly enough, it was only in Vilnius that I undertook satellite surfing as participant observation, spending time with a young man from Šeduva named Vladas, who had come to the capital to attend prestigious Vilnius University.

Personal Reflection

I knew Vladas from when he was in high school. Though I never taught him (he went to a regional honors school), we used to have long and stimulating conversations in English. By the time of my research, he had graduated from high school with national honors, and was a philology student in Lithuania's top university. In order to make ends meet, he took a job at a small, independent hotel that catered to an international clientele. Among the amenities for the guests (and staff) was the satellite television available in the first-floor lounge. Individual rooms were not equipped with TVs, making this lounge the only place where guests were able to watch television.

First and foremost, hotel management has installed this satellite system to accommodate international clientele. Although the hotel's (Lithuanian) owner lives in Japan, the hotel mostly receives business people from other European countries—particularly Germany and Russia. Vladas can speak Russian fluently, but he is not proficient in German; with these clients, English is the language of compromise. However, in Vilnius, it is common for people to be bi- or even tri-lingual, with the ability to communicate in Lithuanian, Russian, or Polish. And that's before factoring in school-learned languages, such as English or French.

Vladas works overnight at the hotel. While he is attentive to clients' needs as they arise, there is a large amount of "down time" inherent in his position to read or study. There is a computer with internet access already paid for by the hotel, which Vladas uses to research for course papers and to read online news.[vii] In addition, there is a satellite television receiver. While he has both a computer and a television at home, the services available at work are an "upgrade" from what he has at his own flat.

When Vladas and his wife Monika lived in a university dormitory, they subscribed to cable television, but were not particularly happy with it. Vladas explained:

> There were too many German programs—and I don't know German. Also, a lot of Russian programs, and I don't like them....They are showing bad—for me, it's bad—not interesting films. Old Russian films and old Hollywood films. These films are stupid: someone is running, fighting, doing illogical things.

The preponderance of German programs Vladas noted points to a cable company with German ties. The coastal region of Lithuania was indeed Prussian in the interwar period, with the Baltic port city of Klaipėda then known as Memel.[viii] Yet outside those doing business with Germans, the percentage of German speakers in Lithuania is quite low. The Russian language, however, is another story altogether, with essentially all adults able to converse in Russian, and significant Russian minorities in major cities. Even still, the choice of programming was off-putting for Vladas. Just as Hollywood is a hegemonic force in cinema globally, Russian film holds a similar position throughout the former Soviet Union. Interestingly, these two cinemas are conflated at the level of action/adventure's generic signifiers (people are "running, fighting") and rejected outright (the films are "stupid" and "illogical"). Ostensibly, access to satellite technologies would allow viewers like Vladas access to non-mainstream texts more to their liking, but instead it appears that market frustrations are largely perpetuated by the multichannel "neo-network" environment.

Adding insult to injury was the way in which non-Russian programming was translated into Russian on the Russian channels. Making a connection with the dubbed voiceovers on early vidotapes available in Lithuania, Vladas points to the absurdly paternal—even authoritarian—voice-over utilized on Russian-language Soviet television news: "And this voice...The stupid intonation of the Russian they use to translate—I've never heard such a voice otherwise. It wants to be important, like *Vrema*. It's impossible to watch." The continuity in tone Vladas describes here, from Soviet news announcer to post-Soviet voiceover "artist," is arresting. This unnatural tone of voice that carries with it echoes of (or at least aspirations of) Russian power, control, and authority has shifted from news to entertainment programming. For Vladas, the draw of satellite programming was the ability to work on different languages—to reinforce his university studies by watching films in French or English language. He said, "I watch for language skills, and to know what they're showing—in the world, in Europe. Not only French, because my French is quite bad, and I can't understand a lot. But when they write what they say [it is better], because to hear what they speak [alone], it's quite impossible."

In a very real sense, then, satellite TV viewing can be an extension of more formal language study. But for this to happen, there had to be French-language programming available with subtitles. More basically, there simply had to be French-language programming *available*. Vladas recalled that, for a while at the hotel, "there was only one French program, and it was Fashion TV. And they were showing all day and night women showing clothes. [Nothing spoken], just annoying music and [models] walking up and down." As far as the network itself was concerned, I have no doubt this *mise-en-scène* was its very reason for being—in fact, by emphasizing visuals over spoken language, Fashion TV could be watched by anyone receiving its signal, regardless of what languages they did or did not speak. For Vladas, though, it was exactly what he *was not* looking for.

Things got better for him, though, with the arrival of the French network TV5 at the hotel. Vladas explained the reason is that "they write in French. They write and speak… Sometimes the film is in English, or Russian or German—but with titles in French." As a university student, satellite television proved to be a boon for Vladas' language skills. It also served as a striking primer to American culture whenever his remote lingered on the PTL network. Vladas now lives as a journalist in the USA, having finished an M.A. at the University of Chicago. Someday we will have to discuss the level of clarity and/or distortion he now sees in those satellite broadcasts.

As we have seen, the multi-channel television environment, often claimed by media scholars as an essential (even quintessential) component of globalization, has emerged unevenly throughout Europe, with transitional Eastern economies as of yet unable to support the higher penetration levels of the West. Further, we have seen in a local context how media globalization can be understood as a function of both access and class. While pointing to the relative lack of presence in rural Lithuania of satellite and cable television delivery technologies, I also want to underscore the recent inroads these technologies have been making in Lithuania. With European Union accession, and greater integration in pan-European markets, the long-term prospects for significantly greater satellite and cable television penetration rates are quite strong. In the years immediately *previous* to accession, however, the vast majority of Lithuanians received their television broadcasts from national networks.

The Persistence of the "Network Era"

Because premium television delivery systems have not yet firmly established themselves throughout Lithuania, domestic broadcasting networks continue to play a crucial role in the country. Indeed, television has become the primary site for advertisers to reach the Lithuanian market (Kaal, 2004). Thus, to take a closer look at Lithuania's primary television networks is to take a closer look at the economic engine fuelling the country's market shift. At the same time, such a move also offers insight into the precarious balance being negotiated throughout Europe between economic and cultural imperatives. As in much of Western Europe, Lithuania is only in its second decade of commercial television, with neo-liberalist loosening of broadcast regulation opening the airwaves to market capital.

Perhaps unsurprisingly, ownership of terrestrial Lithuanian commercial networks has consolidated into an oligopoly, as it has throughout the developed West. Herman and McChesney (1997) offer an articulate and persuasive picture of the dangers of media consolidation—not the least of which being the ways in which media becomes less a tool for democracy than a tool for global corporate capital. However, when we think about how globalization works culturally, we should use their insights as a starting point, rather than as a conclusion. That is, their narrative does effectively demonstrate that the mass media have shifted from a (relatively) democratic pluralism to an undemocratic consolidation, thus universalizing an evolution that was site-specific to the US, Canada, and much of Western Europe.

After all, in the formerly socialist part of Europe, the post-1989 period has seen much *broader* ownership distribution. This is no mere irony: the March 1990 Lithuanian declaration of independence (followed by the collapse of the USSR in August 1991) broke the Party's monopoly on media control. I want to be careful not to paint an overly rosy picture here: monopoly has been replaced by oligopoly (rather than pluralism), with all of its attendant problems. However, increased consolidation in the era of globalization can be fruitfully seen as a continuation of earlier Western media ownership patterns, making the current situation more of a persistence of corporate modernism than some new economic paradigm.

We must remember that in the West, oligopoly has been the rule since the 1930s in motion pictures and radio, and the 1940s in television. Rather than shrugging off a false media utopia of centralized, benevolent control for the true utopia of market choice, Eastern Europe finds itself grappling with a set of regulatory issues that, while new to the region, have vexed the West throughout the 20th Century.

Thus, while the situation in Lithuania may not be ideal by any stretch of the imagination, it has achieved a level of parity with the West. In fact, the evolution of the Lithuanian network television market offers examples of several strategies of network positioning within the global marketplace. Before exploring the ways in which commercial networks have positioned themselves within Lithuania, however, we need to understand the place of public broadcasting in the nation in both its post-Soviet and pan-European contexts.

With the collapse of Soviet power, state broadcaster *Lietuvos televizija* (formerly LTV, now LT) held a brief *de facto* monopoly in Lithuania. However, as neo-liberalist policies took hold, commercial broadcasters took their place over the airwaves and in Lithuanian living rooms. In quick succession, several private broadcast networks entered the market (see below). As in Scandinavia, for example, commercial networks are a relatively recent phenomenon in Lithuania and in the Baltic States; these networks have managed to change the "rules of the game" regarding the financial support for programming. State broadcasters continue to attempt to fulfill "public service" mandates, while also raising a significant portion of their budget via advertising. (As a result, referring to channels like LT1 as "non-commercial" would be a misnomer.)

Formed initially as a tertiary-language "local" network, Lithuanian Television is the successor to the republic-level television that the Soviets put in place in the 1950s. The republic-level broadcaster played a galvanizing role in the *Sąjūdis* movement in the latter half of the 1980s, and increasingly continued to do so once Lithuania declared its re-independence. With this declaration— unrecognized, of course, by Soviet authorities—state television became a primary means by which *Sąjūdis* could communicate with its public. Soon enough, Lithuanian television became not simply an ideological battleground, but, as my opening comments in this chapter indicated, a literal one.

Challenges

However, from the beginning of re-independence, threats came not only from Soviet shock troops, but also from severe economic challenges. Funding that had flowed freely from Moscow in the Soviet era quickly evaporated. Even after the Soviet collapse, *Lietuvos televizija* seems to have perpetually struggled to procure and maintain funding. Unprecedented simultaneous political, economic, and social transitions within the country were certainly central to LT's budgetary woes. But what must also be factored into this equation is the lack of political will to separate the state broadcaster from dependency on government grants and aid. Or, to put it another way, regardless of which parties have controlled parliament, it has made political sense to keep state broadcasting on the proverbial short leash. For instance, during former Lithuanian Communist Party chairman

Algirdas Brazauskas' presidency, the 1996 Law on Lithuanian National Radio and Television legislated a politically appointed council to oversee state broadcasting. Four years later, in the midst of former Bush cabinet appointee Valdas Adamkus' first term, the law was reconsidered but not rescinded.[ix] However, the efficacy of such a move has certainly lessened with the introduction over the past decade of commercial broadcasting. Indeed, in 1995 Lithuania lost what was essentially a monopoly in local-language programming with the introduction of commercial television. Along with this major development, of course, came new questions regarding the ways in which state TV should raise its budget. Specifically, this was a matter of advertising revenue.

Of course, Lithuanian state television is not alone in grappling with such questions. In fact, a closer look at the ways in which various European nations have negotiated issues regarding their own budgets is striking in the very range of solutions in play. One of the ongoing discussions surrounding LT for over a decade has been the question of securing long-term funding through a license fee structure. With this arrangement, every television owner pays a regular fee that is distributed back to state broadcasters. For American readers, perhaps the best-known example of the license fee structure is that of the BBC; while the network is not able to gain additional revenue through advertising, it has succeeded in branding itself globally, successfully exporting programming as well as entire network platforms (e.g., BBC America). By contrast, Sweden's TVE, which is also not allowed to advertise, is nearly entirely dependent on license fees for their operating budget. Rather than through such licensing agreements, Lithuanian Television receives the majority of its budget through government grants.

The crucial difference between license fees and government grants, of course—and the reason why the funding structure is so problematic for the LRTV generally—is that government funding remains contingent on the annual budget allocation of the Lithuanian *seimas* (parliament). License fees, once initiated and properly collected, can be a regular source of revenue that sidesteps the question of editorial oversight. With direct funding, however, the parliament maintains a level of power (be it implicit or explicit) over the network that it would cede under a licensing structure. This leaves the state broadcaster vulnerable not only to indirect pressure, but also to direct political salvos (as seen in the US in the most recent 2005 debates over "balance" on PBS). The dilemma is that not only is parliament reluctant to give up this power, but the general public (those who vote in *seimas* parliamentarians) is reticent to begin directly paying for something that used to be "free." Certainly, the public previously paid for the LRTV indirectly through taxes, but the addition of a direct tax is clearly one that has little political momentum.

Several neo-liberalist arguments regarding public broadcast funding require discussion in this context. One line of reasoning is that, counter to the UK/Sweden model, public networks should utilize advertising to decrease the amount of government funding. For example, a full 40% of the France 2 budget comes from advertising (nearly all the rest comes from license fees). Unlike France 2, however, Lithuania's state broadcaster LRTV manages to earn just over half that (20.4%) (Iosifidis, et. al, 2005). Like its commercial rivals, Lithuanian state television is forced to fight for advertising dollars in a relatively small, less-than-affluent market. Without the linguistic advantages and home-market strength of the BBC, it is particularly difficult for LT to make significant inroads against commercial networks in terms of market share. Also not to be downplayed is the lack of any real public service imperative for the commercial networks. This means that while LT must conform to various government mandates to retain the funding it manages to secure, it has a distinct disadvantage against commercial networks in attracting advertisers. Thus, while LT remains "important," it finds itself more and more on the sidelines in the marketplace.

In this sense, the clear market leaders within Lithuania are networks with very different histories and organizational structures: LNK and TV3. LNK has branded itself as the independent national commercial network, emphasizing initially local-language fare. TV3 is organized around what I call an "economy of scale" model, with a network of other TV3s in Estonia, Latvia, and throughout Scandinavia to share production and distribution costs. LNK has built its brand through in-house production, while TV3 devotes a greater percentage of its broadcast schedule to foreign programming. The structure of these networks offers different viable models for small-nation television in the era of globalization.

To recap this section, low cable and satellite penetration rates have combined with a rich advertising market to solidify and consolidate the position of network television in Lithuania. The top commercial networks TV3 and LNK have employed complementary organizational and programming strategies that have made them the top Lithuanian networks. State-run Lithuanian Television, on the other hand, has been saddled with a budgetary structure that places it under direct budgetary control of the parliament for most of its funding, and requires it to compete for advertising revenue for the rest. On the whole, the current oligopoly in the nation's network broadcasting places Lithuania in a situation similar to that found throughout Europe—for Eastern Europe, even oligopoly has to be seen as something of an improvement on decades of Soviet state monopoly. The future may be a multi-channel environment facilitated by satellite and cable, but (at least for now) Lithuanian television remains in "network era."

Just as advertisers have a vested interest in reaching customers while minimizing costs, television producers (who are in the business of selling audiences to advertisers) have an imperative to structure production budgets to ensure profit margins. With its combination of low production costs and high viewer interest, "reality television" programming has become an answer to both imperatives. While we can speak of "reality TV" as a global programming strategy, it is important to account for the ways in which national and/or regional context inflect the formula. A close look at the variation within locally produced "reality" shows, and the ways in which they are produced and consumed, underscores the continued, contested cultural heterogeneity of global television.

Global Programming, National Programmers: "Reality Television" in Lithuania

In the past decade, "reality television" has received increasingly broad critical attention. Not only has it been a breathtaking industrial phenomenon, it has also opened up critical space to think about the ways in which notions of "reality" (like notions of the nation) are constructed. While news and public affairs programming have been a part of the medium since its inception, the past decade's wave of reality programming has been qualitatively different. Keeping elements of newsgathering *verite*, yet utilizing them for entertainment rather than information, networks have been able to produce shows with miniscule budgets and eye-popping ratings.[x]

Any documentary project is "mediated" in the sense that there are always people making decisions regarding elements of narrative, *mise-en-scène*, cinematography, editing, and sound. These are elements that define any work of film or television, including the genre of "reality television" which has gained such ascendance in the past decade. Thus, "reality TV" is a particularly interesting object of critical inquiry; its connotations of unmediated truth call on us all the more to scrutinize how this "truth" is produced and articulated. In relation to Lithuanian reality television, we might ask several questions. What are some of the different ways Lithuanian "reality television" is constructed? What are the ties between its particular industrial background and the finished product? How differently has state television dealt with this phenomenon? Further, how are both the nation and the viewer being constructed by these programs? What is the tie between such constructions and the shows' industrial context? To address these questions, let's look at three different Lithuanian reality programs: *Atleisk*, *Klausimėlis*, and *Fizz Superstar*.

One of the most consistently popular programs during the research period in Lithuania was LNK's *Atleisk* (*Forgive Me*). Each weekly, hour-long program usually contains three segments that follow a standard format. Before a studio audience, one of two hosts introduces a guest or guests, and their emotional story is explicated. Characteristically, they are looking for lost relations, and we learn the history behind this separation. The *Atleisk* crew brings flowers to the lost subject, though they do not tell at first who the flowers are from—just that they are from someone they haven't seen in a long time. Might they guess who they are from? Meanwhile, there is an inset box with a reaction from the original studio guest(s), seeing this person for the first time in years. Once this clip ends, there is another short discussion with the studio guest(s), including whether or not they have come to the studio to reunite, and what that might mean for them. Nearly always, the 'lost' subject is indeed on the other side of the door, and the family is reunited. Almost always, the producers cut away to the studio audience reacting to this reunion, a shot which is frequently composed of an abundance of both smiles and tears. A brief dénouement with the reunited family follows, wrapped up by direct address to the camera/audience by the host.

On one level, *Atleisk* is about reuniting families—kids searching for parents or vice versa, siblings looking for one another. The program essentially ignores romance, explicitly setting its sights on reuniting *families*. On a more symbolic level, I believe the program is serving as a public forum, giving a national audience the opportunity to grapple with a range of issues, including several that were taboo under Soviet rule: widespread government detention, poverty, alcoholism, orphaned and/or abandoned children, and others.

These social problems are intricately involved with political and economic woes of the past 60 years: occupations (Soviet as well as Nazi), Stalin-era deportations, the multiple restructurings (and ultimate collapse) of the Soviet economy, widespread bank failure in the early years of re-independence, the gutting of the collective farm system leading to widespread rural unemployment, and the 1998 Russian ruble collapse.

In his book *Freaks Talk Back: Tabloid Talk Shows and Sexual Nonconformity*, Joshua Gamson (1998) argues that tabloid TV offers a public space in which counter-hegemonic identity positions are articulated, inducing society to grapple with sexual identities outside proscribed monogamous heterosexual boundaries. For my work here, I am interested in expanding Gamson's notion of talk TV offering a public space for the potentially liberating discussion of 'taboo' subjects to the post-socialist Lithuanian context, in which the "freaks," as it were, are the families that were directly or indirectly shattered as a result of the last half-century. Once the dialogue begins, the sheer amount of these "freaks"—or trauma victims—is staggering.

As a public forum in Lithuania, *Atleisk* invokes (if Peter Brooks [1976] and Benedict Anderson [1991]will forgive me) what I will call a *melodramatic imagined community*. *Atleisk* works as melodrama—specifically as a family melodrama—asking viewers to extrapolate this family's story as a collective story, a national story. A family's forgiveness becomes a collective healing process. In *The Melodramatic Imagination*, Brooks argues, "Melodrama represents both the urge towards resacralization and the impossibility of conceiving sacrilization other than in personal terms" (16). He later continues, "Melodrama is indeed, typically, not only a moralistic drama but the drama of morality: it strives to find, to articulate, to demonstrate, to 'prove' the existence of a moral universe which, though put into question, masked by villainy and perversions of judgment, does exist and can be made to assert its presence and its categorical force among men" (20). The personal is not only political, but is here understood as the locus from which righteousness, forgiveness, and salvation, spring, and the notion of justice might be reasserted. Brooks is speaking from a position of Western society that has secularized gradually ("naturally"?). Now consider a community that was strongly Roman Catholic, that endured a half-century of Soviet occupation, that saw its national cathedral turned into a state Museum of Atheism, that had agents reporting who visited the still functioning village churches, and you can begin to see the potential societal function of melodrama as a resacralizing, national force in the post-Soviet era.

I became interested in *Atleisk* after watching it several times with my interviewees. I was struck by the pathos, not only on screen, but also in these viewers. However, I should mention that I often felt somehow uncomfortable watching this show—that I was witnessing highly personal moments to which I should perhaps not be privy. What I have surmised after talking further to those with whom I watched *Atleisk*, was that, while I might have sympathy for the families, the (intended) Lithuanian audience experienced a feeling closer to empathy, a shared catharsis. I hear stories like the one I just described for you, and I catch myself muttering, "I can't imagine." And they nod with resignation, as if to say "sure, of course for you it's hard to understand."

The goal here is not to argue that these reality programs are an inherently progressive force in Lithuania. They offer the potential of a public sphere in which previously taboo subjects are being addressed, but it is important to underscore the fact that these programs are re-reading these tragedies within frameworks understood as national (and Christian) in character. What's being re-inscribed here is the primacy of the family, and by extrapolation the Lithuanian nation, coming back together after having been ripped asunder by 'foreign' powers. The forgiveness being asked for is that of parent to child, or sibling to sibling. What we are *not* seeing any discussion of here is that of reuniting lost loves. This is not only true of gay and lesbian couples (completely off the radar) but also heterosexual couples, whether married or not. Thus, the ideal posited by the program is an ideal of *familial* over *romantic* love. This is why it is so interesting to look at the program as an example of family melodrama. Nor is this a forum for thinking about the Lithuanian nation as not simply a victim of violence, but also a perpetrator of it. It's unlikely, for instance, that the daughter of someone who took part in the infamous "Kaunas Garage massacre" would reach out to the granddaughter of one of the victims now living abroad.[xi]

In *Atleisk*, Lithuanians are reuniting with other Lithuanians, asking (and receiving) forgiveness for losing contact. However, this is no 'truth and reconciliation commission' hearing—we have no former heads of the Lithuanian SSR apologizing to the widows and children of political exiles, no Moscow heads taking responsibility for the 1991 OMON attacks described at the beginning of this chapter. Nor do we have any accounting by Lithuanians for any violence they might have inflicted on others, either during or after World War II. Thus, the program retains the notion of Lithuania as a martyr nation. The work *Atleisk* does in terms of offering national catharsis for a devastating history is important, but we must also keep in mind those the program will never show—those who may in fact have the most to be forgiven for.

If *Atleisk* operates with a degree of populism, Lithuanian Television's *Klausimėlis* (*A Little Question*) carries itself with an air of paternalism. The program presents a picture of reality of which the populace is largely ignorant, requiring experts to set the record straight. The implication, of course, is that Lithuania *needs* the knowledge and expertise the state broadcaster offers. *Klausimėlis* positions interviewees largely as bumpkins and ignoramuses. Part of the pleasure derived from watching the show comes from the subject position the show offers the viewer: separated from the interviewees, *better* or *higher*. The contrast with *Atleisk* is stark: rather than a collective trauma being dealt with collectively (if presented on an individual level), here we witness collective cultural and historical amnesia in the form of a torrent of responses ranging from the nearly accurate to the wildly inaccurate.

While questions central to Lithuanian statehood are a staple on *Klausimėlis*, broader questions of cultural importance are posed as well. One episode (aired in 2002) asked participants what they know about Mona Lisa, without expressly referring to the enigmatic Leonardo da Vinci portrait. Again, we are presented with a range of wild guesses regarding to whom the interviewer is referring, including both the Queen of England and the future Queen of America. Ostensibly, those watching state TV already know this "elementary" fact, placing viewers in a similarly knowing (smug?) position as the week's guest expert.

The way this program frames power relationships is important: respondents offer up inaccurate (if not downright incoherent) responses to seemingly simple questions, underscoring the need for authority figures to step in and correctly discuss the issue at hand. Thus, the show invites its audience to identify *not* with the reality of the "man on the street," but the informed reality of the expert who corrects and chides these folks. The show, then, has its viewers relate to the network as a source of expert material, the place where social and cultural knowledge is to be found. Ostensibly the public network for the Lithuanian populace, Lithuanian Television in fact bares elitist contempt for this same public through programs as such.

If *Atleisk* (and to a lesser extent, *Klausimėlis*) provides a forum for Lithuanians to individually and collectively work through their past, other "reality" programming offers a space within which to work through their present moment—in particular, the geopolitical moment in which the nation was on the cusp of EU and NATO accession. Looking back at the pre-accession years from a post-2004 vantage point, the very real contingency of accession can be lost. Indeed, the "big bang" in which both organizations added a large number of additional nations simultaneously, obscures the widely felt notion that the various candidate states were competing with one another for a potentially limited number of slots. It is this very lack of clarity of the "rules of the game" that caused considerable anxiety throughout the region—anxiety that manifested itself in seemingly curious, seemingly innocuous, places. (Elsewhere, I have argued that the Eurovision Song Contest is just such a place—see Ingvoldstad, 2007.) Serialized contests and game shows also became a site where pre-accession anxieties played out, as they often pitted contestants from the three Baltic States against one another. It was progress, albeit measured: less than a decade earlier, television framed, articulated, and fanned ethnic difference in the former Yugoslavia in the march to civil war (see Gow et. al, 1996); here, TV used not dissimilar framing devices in the former Soviet Baltic to produce cost-efficient programming that could work in several markets simultaneously. A multi-national song contest like *Fizz Superstar* asks very different things from its viewers, though it still serves as a remarkable site for understanding the dynamics and pressures of post-socialist transition.

Global Genre

When I returned to Lithuania for follow-up research in Summer 2002, the *Fizz Superstar* contest (broadcast on LNK) was reaching its climax.[xii] The contest had been running a month, eliminating all but the final contestants. Though I arrived *in medias res*, it was clear something interesting was going on. People were talking a lot about the show—not just friends and discussants who were familiar with my research interests, but also people I met my first week back, who asked if I'd been following the show. I was intrigued, but I had also missed every show up to this point, and didn't even realize which night the finals were to be broadcast.

The week of *Joninės* (summer solstice), a number of friends and I got together for a party at Vaidas and Vilė's flat—participant observation research at its best. The television was turned on at some point for background noise and visuals, as the kids were starting to get squirrelish. Vaidas finds a children's program with which the youngest (not quite two years old) is completely enraptured. After this, the Lithuanian version of *Who Wants To Be a Millionaire?* comes on (only with the lighting scheme of *The Weakest Link*). Then, finally, it is the finals for *Fizz Superstar*.

The Swedish division of Universal Records is backing this talent contest/pan-Baltic TV spectacle, roughly based on the British hit *Pop Idol* (soon after imported to the USA as *American Idol*).[xiii] Singers from Lithuania, Latvia, and Estonia compete against one another, making the contest take on nationalist overtones: the singers come to personify their nation in the same way as Olympic contestants. Three hosts (one from each country) co-present the finals. However, whereas in Eurovision the two presenters are both from the same (host) country but address each other in English and French, here each host speaks in her or his own native language and appears to not even understand the others. In addition, there are no titles or voiceovers for the Latvian or Estonian speaker, making them indecipherable to the Lithuanian audience. Sensing the confusion, the Lithuanian host, pop singer and media journalist Marijonas Mikutavičius, clearly deviated from the script when explaining that "*of course* this time we *have* to win and we *will* win (winks), right friends?"

There were several reasons for this ironically willful optimism. With six of ten finalists from Lithuania, sheer numbers were on their side. However, to understand the sense of bitter urgency undergirding that optimism, one needs to be conversant with some recent low moments in Lithuanian popular culture. "We *have* to win," Vaidas asserts. "Really!" adds his sister Inga. "We lost at Eurovision, we lost in basketball, we lost in football. What else?" Vilė doesn't miss a beat. "*Robinsonai*. The Olympics." Let me briefly unpack this conversation.

The 2002 Eurovision Song Contest debacle for Lithuania involved their entrant Aivaras and his forever-berated beret. This contestant made an abysmal showing, placing so low as to eliminate the nation from competition the subsequent year (see Ingvoldstad, 2007). This happened at the contest in Estonia (winners in 2001) in which a Latvian singer emerged with top honors for 2002. With her basketball reference, Inga is either referring to the two narrow losses to the USA at the Olympics, or the bitter loss to Latvia in the qualifying rounds of the World Basketball Championships. The football reference points to Lithuania's failure to qualify (yet again) for the 2002 World Cup. *Robinsonai* (*The Robinsons*, as in *The Swiss Family Robinson*) was an early *Survivor* adaptation in Fall 2001 in which contestants from all three Baltic States competed in Estonia. Lithuanians failed to win either that year or in the subsequent year's contest, located in the South Pacific. Finally, the Olympics reference cites either the losses to Team USA in basketball once again or the more recent 2002 Winter Olympics in which Lithuania was denied its only medal (in ice dancing) in the midst of judge-fixing allegations, similar to that of the pairs skating controversy that erupted that same year. But let's return to the contest at hand. Each contestant sings a cover of a popular song (e.g., Robbie Williams' "Millennium," Shakira's "Whenever, Wherever"). All songs are in English, and none are originals—a stark reminder of the rules of the game for artists attempting to break out of their native markets with regional, pan-European, or global deals. What is the result? A fifteen-year-old Estonian girl walks off with top marks and a newly minted contract for her winning rendition of Nelly Furtato's "I'm Like a Bird." The Lithuanians I am watching with are left with the cold comfort of linking arms and spontaneously reworking an old Queen anthem: "We are the *losers!*"

Lithuania has a series of its own national contests and awards programs functioning in a way similar to that of the Grammys or *American Idol* in their celebration of home-grown talent. However, one of the things that is remarkable about contests like *Fizz Superstar* or Eurovision is that their multinational and regional geographic parameters are set by producers. Universal, like the rest of the "Big Five" music conglomerates, has treated Estonia, Latvia, and Lithuania as a single market to sell to and possibly to recruit talent from. There are some legitimate historic and logistic reasons for this. After all, the three nations (who at that time were Soviet republics) worked together for independence from Moscow in the late 1980s and early 1990s. Perhaps even more to the point, the population of the Baltic States combined is smaller than that of the Czech Republic, and approximately one-fourth that of Poland. With that said, there are significant linguistic and cultural differences between the Baltic States as well. Upon the collapse of the USSR, the three states traveled different, albeit parallel, paths in the ensuing decade of the 1990s. Once negotiations to enter the EU and NATO began in earnest, the rules of the game were such that, at times, it felt like nations were competing against one another for a limited number of spaces, rather than trying to meet a set of objective criteria. By 2002, there was no love lost between Lithuanians and the Estonian government after an Estonian minister asserted that he represented a *Scandinavian* (not *Baltic*) country.

Implicitly, the message was that Estonia was Western and ready for EU accession while Latvia and Lithuania were not. This study finds regional, transatlantic, and global organizations tending to frame these states as being inherently similar (post-socialist transition markets, with a Soviet military legacy); this, in turn, given the perceived "rules of the game" for EU and NATO accession, prompt the aspiring nations to differentiate themselves from the other "contestants." We see a similar zero-sum game played out here in the reactions of a local Lithuanian audience to the *Fizz Superstar* competition. By replicating larger geo-political contests, the program becomes a means to collectively articulate fears, frustrations, and perhaps resignations generated as a result of the current political and economic environment.

Importantly, though, along with the defeatism there is playfulness, a sense that tomorrow might still be different. Indeed, in 2004, over a dozen years after declaring re-independence from the USSR, Lithuania (along with the other two Baltic states) did indeed formally join both the EU and NATO. Having "returned to Europe" to use a phrase coined by Timothy Garton Ash (1990), Lithuanians now wonder what might come next.[xiv]

Conclusion and Summary

This discussion of reality television articulates how a global genre (or, if you like, a global *mode*) functions on and is articulated by the national imaginary. With relatively low cable and satellite penetration rates, and therefore with global channels and networks making muted impact in Lithuania, the importance of national television networks remains high. Indeed, with television receiving the majority of ad spending, Lithuanian networks are engines for economic reform. Of course, they also provide a crucial means of imagining and negotiating the nation. Throughout this chapter, I have been making a case for the notion of *small-nation globalization*. Differentiation and power allocation (rather than homogenization and egalitarianism) are in play with a particular geopolitical twist. Lithuania's largely rural population has not embraced satellite and cable delivery systems, which in turn has made the nation's national networks that much more important. As an international format that takes on local, national, and regional guises, "reality television" programming in Lithuania also reveals the way uneven, localized ways in which globalization manifests. If *Fizz Superstar* was a site of contestation between Baltic States, symbolically negotiating a collective future, *Atleisk* was a forum through which Lithuania was working through its collective past. Even state TV tried its hand at "reality TV," although *Klausimėlis* was most revealing in terms of how LT pejoratively framed the majority of the nation.

In addition to the ways in which I have discussed television in terms of globalization, I have also made explicit links between TV and post-socialism. While some post-socialist states have embraced new television delivery systems at Western levels, other countries such as Lithuania have been slower to embrace satellite and cable. While national networks maintain their importance in the country, international business dealings are integrating Lithuania into Europe through other means. The case of MTG and their confederation of TV3 channels throughout the Baltic and Scandinavia point to an important way these two European regions are working together—albeit a partnership between Scandinavian ownership and Baltic consumption. The commercialization of the Lithuanian television market, as well as the budgetary crunch of state-run LT points to something of a crisis in post-socialist public television. Finally, I have shown how a global programming strategy—"reality television"—functions and reveals a range of concerns tied to a socialist legacy.

The interplay between television and its Lithuanian audiences from several different vantage points was discussed and articulated. Technological changes in television delivery, rather than a harbinger of universal access, help us see the uneven nature of globalization on a range of levels. The national broadcast networks continue to be popular, although both public and private channels continue to struggle to secure their viability in a volatile market. Television programming itself can be understood as creating a public space around which the past, present, and future are all simultaneously being worked through. By triangulating our understanding by looking from several different viewpoints, we gain a better perspective of a land where, in January 1991, the revolution *was*, in fact, televised.

References and Notes

Anderson, B. (1991). Imagined communities: Reflections of the origin and spread of nationalism (2nd ed.). New York: Verso.

Balcytiene, A. (2002). Lithuanian media—a question of change. In P. Vihalemm (Ed.), Baltic media in transition (pp. 103-134). Tartu: Tartu University Press.

Brooks, P. (1976). The melodramatic imagination: Balzac, Henry James, melodrama, and the mode of excess. Clinton: Colonial Press.

Curtin, M. (1996). On edge: Culture industries in the neo-network era. In A. Ohmann, G. Averill, M. Curtin, D. Shumway, & E. G. Traube (Eds.), Making and selling culture (pp. 181-202). Hanover: Wesleyan University Press.

EAO. (1994/95). Statistical Yearbook 1994/95. Strasbourg: European Audiovisual Observatory. (2004). Statistical Yearbook 2004 (2 volumes). Strasbourg: European Audiovisual Observatory.

Gamson, J. (1998). Freaks talk back: Tabloid talk shows and sexual nonconformity. Chicago: University of Chicago Press.

Garton Ash, T. (1990). The magic lantern: The revolution of '8 witnessed in Warsaw, Budapest, Berlin, and Prague. New York: Random House.

Gow, J., Paterson, R., & Preston, A. (Eds.) (1996). Bosnia by television. London: British Film Institute.

Herman, E. S. & McChesney, R. W. (1997). The Global Media: The new missionaries of global capitalism. Washington: Cassell.

Ingvoldstad, B. (2007). Lithuanian contests and European dreams. In I. Raykoff & R. Deam (Eds.), A song for Europe: popular music and politics in the Eurovision Song Contest (pp. 99-110). Burlington: Ashgate.

Iosifidis, P., Steemers, J., & Wheeler, M. (2005). European Television Industries. London: British Film Institute.

Jaafar, A. (2005). 'Star' lights up auds in Iraq: Talent show offers viewers an escape. Variety Aug. 29- Sept. 4, p. 32.

Kaal, E. (2004). Baltic media advertising market 2003. Retrieved August 3, 2004 from http://www.emor.ee/emg/arhiiv.html?id=1189.

Lieven, A. (1994). The Baltic revolution: Estonia, Latvia, Lithuania and the path to independence (2nd ed.). New Haven: Yale University Press.

Misiunas, R. & Taagepera, R. (1993). The Baltic states: Years of dependence 1940-1990 (expanded and updated ed.). Berkeley: University of California Press.

Saja, K., Rybelis, A., Mickevičius, D., Šimkūnas, Ladukas, Č., & Zibucas, I. (1992). Lithuania 1991.01.13: Documents testimonies comments. Vilnius: State Publishing Center.

Williams, R. (2003). Television: Technology and cultural form (Routledge Classics edition). New York: Routledge Classics.

Other Notes

1. Indeed, with the spheres of influence duly carved, the Nazis began their invasion of Poland just over a week later, on September 1st, 1939, with the Soviets incorporating under duress Lithuania, Latvia, and Estonia into the USSR that next year.

2. I consciously use the passive voice here: a decision was made, but to this day debate rages regarding whom in fact *gave* this order. Gorbachev maintained (and still maintains) that he himself did not, but this only begs the question: who did? If Gorbachev was not in control of these "shock troops," then who was? How in control of the government *was* he, at this point? On the other hand, if Gorbachev, counter to his assertions, *did* order in the "Black Berets," this points to a major (albeit ultimately half-measured) shift to the right, ostensibly to shore up his power base among hard-liners, months before the August 1991 coup. For Kremlin-watchers, the events of 1991 underscored the limits of *perestroika* and *glasnost*, and even brought into question their very long-term viability

3. The events surrounding January 13th have now become family history. My wife, who was in secondary school at the time, recalls how, from her family's apartment window, she could see Soviet soldiers brandishing rifles arriving at the tower. Her father, who was the primary technician for the site, went outside rather than have them conduct a search of the apartment house. While my father-in-law shrugs off any memory of danger from this encounter, my wife remembers being terrified at the thought that troops might shoot her dad as they had the unarmed Vilnius protestors.

4. Several civilians were killed in Riga exactly one week after 13 January, including a cameraman and a production assistant of Latvian documentarist Juris Podnieks. His film *Baltic Requiem* (1991) chronicles both January crackdowns, including the wrenching loss of two friends and colleagues while capturing the attacks on video.

5. Cell phone usage has of course exploded throughout Europe, but I cannot say to what extent telephony infrastructure disrepair contributed to this outside the Baltic States.

6. I was befriended by one family who had a rather large satellite dish that was in disrepair, but they were in no hurry to fix or replace it.

7. At home, Vladas limited his internet usage to email, which was a tactical decision involving not only his access at work, but also the pricing structures of home internet usage in Lithuania.

8. Klaipėda was a part of the Hanseatic League in the Middle Ages, and celebrated its 750th anniversary in 2002.

9. See Aukše Balcytiene (2002) for more discussion of this law within the larger question of media change in Lithuania.

10. The Super Bowl-like atmosphere surrounding the communal viewing of the final installment of the first season of CBS's *Survivor* (2001) is indicative of how galvanizing the format can be. For that matter, the dazzling proliferation of reality shows in its wake, including several programs that recycled former notables of the genre, also underscores the breadth and robust nature of the genre—to say nothing of the profit margins for networks and advertisers alike.

11. For more about the tragic fate of Jews in Lithuania, see Anatol Lieven (1994) and Misiunas and Taagepera (1993).

12. "Fizz" was a new brand of alcoholic drink—sometimes referred to as an "alcopop"—marketed for a young, hip demographic. The drink's English name ostensibly adds to its cachet—as does the English name of the program.

13. This franchise continues to flourish not only in the UK and USA, but also recently in China and Iraq (Jaafar 2005).

14. Among the things that came next, of course was the Second Iraq War of 2003. Lithuania, as a country among "the coalition of the willing," was therefore placed in Defense Secretary Rumsfeld's taxonomy as being a part of "New Europe."

15. This franchise continues to flourish not only in the UK and USA, but also recently in China and Iraq (Jaafar 2005).

16. Among the things that came next, of course was the Second Iraq War of 2003. Lithuania, as a country among "the coalition of the willing," was therefore placed in Defense Secretary Rumsfeld's taxonomy as being a part of "New Europe."

Chapter Seven

Regional and Global Media in the Middle East Challenges Facing Media Organizations In the Era of Convergence

Jabbar A. Al-Obaidi
Bridgewater State University

Organizational Media Tools

Communication technologies are consistently and increasingly changing and with them communication and social and organizational media tools change as well. In the last decade, the printing press, photography, cinematography, radio, internet, and satellite television have catapulted into un-imaginable heights. Whereas they were once at risk for total control by governments, these forms of media and communication tools have broken away and set a new bar on how media and new communication technology can be put to use. This development can be seen in the rate at which Blogging and the use of YouTube have expanded. Further, regional and global media organizations quietly began chitchatting about a new buzzword, convergence in 2000-2001. Bob Salsberg, Chairperson of RTNDA explained, "There is a reason convergence is a buzzword in the industry. Like streams emptying into a river, TV, radio and print are all slowly beginning to merge." (Salsberg 2003). He added, "We are not yet sure where this digital river will flow, but don't sit back while the waters rush past." (Salsberg 2003).

Most leaders of the Middle East appeared to have determined not to sit back while technological changes rush past. The Arab League and other Middle East regional organizations have embraced the newly emerged technological developments in the arena of global media. The regional market is wide and hospitable. Worth noting is the fact that the Middle East region consists of more than twenty countries with a population of more than 400 million of different ethnic backgrounds, six predominant languages, and three key religions. The region embraces rather deep and complex historical, cultural, and political ties. Aware of their mosaic political structures, each individual country has created its own media system and communication pattern.

In addition, each country has adopted and designed an organizational model that each has deemed necessary to answer to their sociopolitical and cultural needs. Since the 1950s, an elaborate media system has developed, and it has expanded over the decades. Interest in building more radio and satellite television facilities appears now to grow bigger and faster. Still, governments stride to do more in the hope of strengthening their connectivity with their audiences within and abroad. Governments and people have come to realize that communication across distance can act as a catalyst for cultural and social changes. They also have come to understand the broader use of media and communication in the area of education, agriculture, politics, and social mobilization.

"The challenge of understanding any kind of cultural transformations is only partially explained by any adopted technology."(Palmer, 2007) In other words, communication technology has been used by Middle East regional organizations and people more as a tool or a conveyer, but not necessarily as an agent for cultural or political analysis. Hence, as political and cultural challenges began to surface, the "hoped-for leapfrog effect" predicted in the 1960s by Schramm and others remained a vague hope. (Neher, 2003) In addition, the expeditious and thorough processes of media and communication convergence have forced organizations to ignore the historical connections between what the developers of communication technology intended it to be used for and the actual selective uses to which it has been applied. Along this line Allen Palmer and G.I. Rochlin argued that developers failed to recognize otherwise that history has been shaped by the form and use of "tools in ways totally unanticipated by the inventors [and], as always, conveniently forgotten." (Rochlin, 1999 & Palmer, 2007) Some governments dealt with this historical development rather differently. The region witnessed a revolution in using the satellite cable television. The later, has worked to strengthen rather than undermine existing regimes as the Arab Gulf ruling elites utilize it to support and enhance non-democratic power structures. In fact the Gulf Cooperation Council GCC is in full support of the new media. However, GCC is still exploring the potential to issue regulations and policies.

Reviewing the proceedings for the media workshop organized by the Center for Contemporary Arab Studies (CCAS) at George Town University showed that the growth of the Internet, for example, in the Middle East was first achieved by business organizations. The Internet was not looked at as tool for doing or developing research in universities and research centers, but as a vehicle for commercial use. However, this approach was reversed, and the Internet is now widely used by schools, universities, and other purposes in the region. Anderson (1996), one of the contributors to the workshop, explained, "It is not too much of a stretch to imagine that the Middle East governments will provide for commerce the infrastructure services and development subsidies that, for cultural and political reasons, they may hesitate to provide for the educational sector." Nevertheless, such infrastructure development has opened the door for more collaboration among educational institutions, media organizations, and the commercial world. (Anderson, 1996)

Consequently, convergence as a term began to be used by most media organizations in 2003. Governments and private sectors engaged heavily in all kind of activities as part of the Middle East information project. Exclusively, it was to bring about a change and to create a new environment for a different kind of convergence in the region. On the Arab world front, the Arab League and ministries of information and culture drew an ambitious plan for the Arab Information Project (AIP). The preliminary purpose of the AIP was to discuss and introduce ways and methods for convergence in the Middle East. An aspect addressed by Evelyn Early, an anthropologist with the US Information Agency at the George Town media workshop organized by CCAS in 1996 stated that radio and television were well-positioned to deal with the convergence issue. (http://aipnew.wordpress.com) The public in the Middle East views television and radio as the main sources of information. In spite of the abundance of communication technologies, this need for television and radio is going to remain for a longer time. Reasons for such a demand are the high rate of illiteracy, financial difficulties, and organizational missteps (http://aipnew.wordpress.com).

Public Interests

The public high interest in radio and television is not unique to the audience in the Middle East. Radio and television are the existing realms of choice in most developing counties. Globally and regionally, radio still has a strong role in conveying information and news and in the discussion of social and political trends and conditions in the region. A quick visit to Middle Eastern rural areas would provide enough evidence to this point. In addition, television still plays the role of a conveyer of ceremony, cultural festivities, and somehow conveys legitimacy on governments. In spite of the growing popularity of the Internet, Middle Eastern people still consider radio and television as their major sources of information, news, education, entertainment, and global views. (http://aipnew.wordpress.com)

Over the period, 2006-2009 governments and local producers managed to overcome the linguistic issue that challenged Arab web designers for years. Brian Whitaker, a journalist from United Kingdom wrote for Al-bab, "For several years it was very difficult to produce web pages in Arabic, which meant that initially Internet use was confined to the education elite who could read European languages." (al-bab.com) The situation has drastically changed since 2005. While working with selective local and global communication enterprises, governments in the Middle East have recognized the importance of political and cultural changes. Internally, governments have seized the opportunity to monopolize the local media while importing new communication technologies and relaxing regulations at the same time. Governments and private sectors have observed and have studied the profiles of media consumption and social impact and have affirmed a pattern of reliance on multiple sources. (http://aipnew.wordpress.com). Fred Huxley from the US Information Agency has argued that people throughout the Middle East region are already multiple multimedia consumers. Almost every member of the family owns at least one mobile phone.

Communication technologies and media outlets have been made to fit into cultural patterns through information formats that draw together content and analysis from different global communication sources or with multimedia as conceived from the deliverer's end. (http://aipnew.wordpress.com). Middle East educators, media professionals, and officials have recognized and understand the need for preparing their media organizations and school curriculums for convergence and its applications. They did not want to stay behind everybody else in the world. RTNDA's chairperson Bob Salsberg explains, "There is a reason convergence is a buzzword in the industry. Like streams emptying into a river, TV, radio and print are all slowly beginning to merge. Media organizations were not sure where this digital river would flow." (Salsberg, 2003)

In spite of the low number of computers, narrow scale of computer networking and high prices for getting an Internet services, users enjoy receiving almost the same content via their computers, television set, and mobile telephone. Media and communications have converged.

Satellite television is on the rise. This author took many snapshots of the literally hundreds of satellite dishes sitting on the top roofs of houses, equally in wealthy and poor areas in Egypt, Jordan, Tunisia, and Yemen. This trend highlights the interest of the people of the region in getting more information and entertainment programs. It also shows the possibilities available for advertisement and commercial business in the region.

Media Convergence

Media convergence is like communication itself. The ongoing process involves technology, content, and audience. The dictionary offers us the following definition to the term convergence: convergence means "two or more things coming together or the state of having come together toward a common point." According to Jussi Ilmarinen (2005), director of Convergence Marketing and Sales, Networks, Nokia, "there are different elements to convergence, industry convergence, service convergence; terminal convergence or network convergence." He pointed out "all of them are happening at the same time - creating major changes in the communications industry. The change is evolutionary, but they affect existing businesses in many ways."(Ilmarinen, 2005). He added, "When we think about convergence it means added value for the end user." (Ilmarinen, 2005) Moreover, MIT Professor Henry Jenkins has described five processes of convergence: (web.mit.edu, Jenkins, 2001 & Tanner and Duhé, 2005)

-Technological convergence that involves process for digitization of information and images that caused information to expand and to travel fast across platforms to all corners of the planet.

-Social convergence that enables consumers' multitasking strategies for navigating an unlimited digitized information environment.

-Economic convergence facilitates the process of integrating many forms of entertainment industry, sport, music, film, and countless other sectors. This development resulted in the "restructuring of cultural production around 'synergies,' and thus the transmedia exploitation of branded properties-Pokémon, Harry Potter, Tomb Raider, Star Wars."

-Cultural convergence provides diverse content and allows audience to share and consume the information on individual and group levels. It also encourages consumers to be more creative in selecting the package of entertainment and information.

-Global convergence creates a receptive international environment that provides more opportunities for communities around the globe. (web.mit.edu, Jenkins, 2001 & Tanner and Duhé, 2005)

Tanner and Duhé (2005) showed significant discrepancies among educators and media professionals when it comes to the issue of understanding the global meaning of media convergence. They also indicated, "There was much less agreement between educators and news directors as to what is considered convergence." (Tanner & Duhé, 2005) Moreover, Tanner and Duhé pointed out that "nine of ten educators agreed that convergence was being practiced when different mediums share their staff and when one fully integrated newsroom acts as an information pool for all forms of media." (Tanner and Duhé, 2005) In addition, they found "less than half of the news directors included the use of a fully integrated newsroom in their definition of convergence and six of ten said the sharing of staff was considered convergence." (Tanner &Duhé, 2005)

As a period of economic and information openness, the period of 2003-2007 gave birth to sort of an unrestrained media convergence. Newspapers, publishing houses, and satellite television seemed to have embraced media convergence, and certainly have developed successful cross-media models for press, online, mobile, and broadcast. Media organizations in Kuwait, Qatar, United Arab Emirates, Turkey, Israel, and Lebanon illustrate the evolution of their different media as they adapted to emerging communication technologies. Al-Jazeera, LBC, and Al-Arabiya aired many programs in 2006-2008 discussing media convergence and global media. Participants, including journalists, writers and broadcasters, asserted that global media present no political or cultural threats if the Middle East media offer good content. They also agreed that journalistic tradition is alive and well in the region despite changes in communication technologies. Practically, convergence becomes a reality in the region. In 2008, companies and media organizations applied its applications in programs like sports, news, documentaries, and entertainment.

Global Phenomenon

Governments and media organizations in the Middle East have finally conceded that the Internet is a global phenomenon. They also agreed that it brings a special regional profile. Dabbagh Information Technology in Dubai estimates that less than one percent of households in the Arab world subscribe to Internet services, rising to three percent in some Arab Gulf countries (Oman, Kuwait, Qatar, Saudi Arabia, United Arab Emirates, and Bahrain). Field surveys put the overall growth rates in the low double digits. (Anderson & Eickelman, 2008)

Yet, the Middle East airwaves is electronically penetrated by numerous radio and TV satellite signals that originate from different parts of the world. The majority comes from within the region. According to Yahya R. Kamalipour these communication channels—many of them controversial—along with the Internet, facsimiles, and telephones have created a unique opportunity for the region, to openly discuss and debate a slew of political, cultural, and social issues on the global stage. (Kamalipour, 2007) Consequently, two essential questions surface: To what extent does the practice of convergence actually happen within media organizations in the Middle East, and what are the challenges facing the Middle Eastern media organizations in the era of convergence?

Both governments and private media owners have adopted a descriptive approach to deal with these questions. They also have looked at the relevant findings made available by the United Nations, the European Union, and media organizations in the United States. Countries like Qatar, Egypt, United Arab Emirates, Lebanon, and Turkey formed their own study groups to review relevant literature covering signs of convergence in the Middle East. Market entry, financial structures and fees, and political decisions associated with the promulgation of new trends for media were considered.

Challenges

The main challenges facing media organizations in the Middle East in the era of convergence and global outreach include the power of global media organizations. Preliminary examinations of the policies and structures of media organizations in the Middle East hit an alarm bell. The general structures of media organizations and current policies do not seem to promote a well-established distribution system that allows the flow of diversified media content. Research also shows the lack of a diversified local or regional content that can compete with admittedly very powerful and largely sophisticated global media organizations. This program content of global media has managed to reach out to and stake a claim on different audiences in the Middle East. It is worth noting that this circumstance is not necessarily a unique cultural occurrence only in the Middle East. As an international issue, countries must work together to deal with it. Together, they can reach a reasonable balance between local and global needs. Consequently, a few states in the region began acquiring more local television and radio programming to keep audiences tuned in. José Roberto Marinho addressed the World Summit on the Information Society (2005):

> *In the past, the greatest threat to the freedom and pluralism of the media came from authoritarian governments in many countries. Currently, this*

same threat (which still exists) has been added another: the need for balance in relation to the power of the global media organizations. This threat has escalated with the convergence of the media and telecommunications companies. One of the most important challenges we increasingly face is to ensure that the diversified content of media companies can flow freely along the content distribution channels.(WEMF, 2005.)

Marinho recognized three conditions for free global media to prevail: First, international media giants cannot offset national and local media. Second, a rich portfolio of media options should be available for to public, with no centralized guidance. Third, telecommunication companies should not be allowed to control media companies."(WEMF, 2005) A globalized media organization "not only must do business internationally but also must have a corporate culture and value system that allow it to move its resources anywhere in the world to achieve the greatest competitive advantages" (Rhinesmith, 1996) Nevertheless, the concept of corporate culture in the Middle East remains fatuous, and needs more time to mature.

Challenges facing media organizations in the Middle East in the era of convergence and global outreach include political conditions and media regulations. Global media and the era of convergence generated a change in the area of politics and media regulations. In this respect, media witnessed more freedom and less of governmental interference. This development was enforced "by increasingly open contest over the authoritative use of the symbolic language of Islam. New and increasingly accessible modes of communication have made these contests increasingly global." (Eickelman & Anderson, 2003) The rigidity of political conditions has been relaxed as well. This came as a direct result from the "access to contemporary forms of communication that range from the press and broadcast media to fax machines and audio-and videocassettes and from the telephone to the Internet." (Eickelman & Anderson, 2003). In this sense, media convergence has broadened up the cultural public sphere and political public dialogue. Moreover, Marinho called for the necessity to "distinguish between communication, a social fact, and distribution, and a physical infrastructure." (WEMF, 2005)

In addition, "the latest technological facilities and convergence in the media sector cannot blind us to the different needs, concerns and regulations which should govern each one of these fields. Telecommunication and content distribution channels are services and tools that create enormous possibilities for well-being and an improved quality of life."(WEMF, 2005) In the face of this technological development, the state in the Middle East is really too powerless to limit the use of the Internet or mobile phones, texting, Facebook, MySpace, and Twittering, and other communication technologies without disrupting the social order, the economy, and the marketplace. It is important to note that from "Indonesia to Morocco, email and the Internet foster new and rapid forms of communication and coordination for religion" and politics and commerce. (Eickelman & Anderson, 2003). Except for Israel, Turkey, Lebanon, and Iraq (post April 9, 2003), most governments still own radio and television organizations as well as manage the general policies, regulations, and financial affairs of those media organisations. However, some of the phone networks and Internet services turned to the private sector in 2007.

Challenges facing in the Middle Eastern media organizations include financial challenges. In the flush of the expansion of the media industry and the prosperity of communication technology, most of the Middle Eastern states have been attempting to ride the wave of progress and modernization. Turkey, Israel, Qatar, the United Arab Emirates are among the first pioneers in joining the race for media convergence. Other countries are trying to engaging themselves in economic reforms and open markets. Yet, "major changes in international financial markets are particularly challenging to the Middle East." (Henry & Springborg, 2001) The financial challenges in the Middle East will continue unless governments show a willingness to introduce "an entirely new model of political, economic, and physical reconstruction." (Henry & Springborg, 2001)

Challenges facing Middle East media organizations include limitations of the freedom of expression and the flow of information: With the exception of Israel, Turkey, and Lebanon, Iraq, the Middle Eastern countries still maintain tough measures against the flow of information, limiting freedom of the press, harassing civil societies, pressuring private media organizations, and stifling individual freedoms. Hassan Mohamed Hamed called on the governments and private sectors to:

A. *"Forge ahead to activate and enable broadcasting media institutions to cope with new forms of digital, transnational, decentralized and interactive broadcasting media by expanding public access, encouraging free flow of information and a wider and better balanced dissemination of information." (WEMF, 2005)*

B. Allow *"access to information, respect for human rights; freedom of expression; freedom of the press and strengthening the forces of democracy."*

C. National and local broadcasting media systems *"should make every effort to address public needs as well as to make information affordable to the majority, free of charge or at a minimum charge." WEMF, 2005).*

D. Cultural diversity: Hassan Mohamed Hamed stated *"Media diversity and a pluralistic press should be encouraged and supported reflecting the widest possible range of opinion and participation within the community."(WEMF 2005)*

Challenges facing media organizations in the Middle East include 'seeking over receiving.' Use of the Internet in the Middle East region demonstrated a noticeable increase in 2003-2008. The audiences, especially younger people, have remove themselves from being in the receiving line to take a better position where they can make and seek the information they are interested in. The gatekeepers and official censors are not pleased with this development, but virtually can do nothing to stop it. The local authorities cannot overcome this challenge and see it as absolutely out of control.

Challenges facing Middle East media organizations include the growth of diverse culture in the Middle East. An early result of the openness to the content and techniques of global media produced a more diverse radio and television media culture, including program content permeated by political reporting and ideological commentary. Such content is highly demanded by the audience in the region. Global and regional media seemed to grow hand in hand in the Middle East. Both appeared to facilitate a journalism that is able to keep up with the traditional and new political culture on which it reports. The newly established regional media began to move closely to the audience by bringing issues that are more important into public discourse and by facilitating a broader-based journalism. In the way it is spreading around, new media in the Middle East is equated by some media critiques to the revolution of the videocassette recordings circulated in the region in the 1970s. As a new technology for its time, it was not only part of the sermons of prominent preachers but also a device for folk music and recitations. Videocassettes were used to record local and even neighborhood radio and television stations to be circulated among different political and religious groups. The use of audio and videocassettes by the late Ayatollah Khomeini of Iran 1976-1979 is only one example to illustrate the importance of any new media. To fast forward, the uprising and demonstration that occurred in Iran after the Iranian election of June 12, 2009 has provided more evidence about the importance of new social media. The embattled government attempted to block the Internet and electronic communication, but the use of new social media exploded and defied censorship and hardships. The New York Times reported "Iranians are blogging, posting to Facebook and, most visibly, coordinating their protests on Twitter, the messaging service. Their activity has increased, not decreased, since the presidential election on Friday and ensuing attempts by the government to restrict or censor their online communications." (New York Times, June 16, 2009) Marinho reminded media and communication experts that "a free media must provide each citizen with both a mirror and a window. In other words, like a mirror, it must ensure that each one has the right to recognize him- or herself in what is seen, heard, and read. This [recognition] engenders a feeling of belonging to society. At the same time, like a window, it must broaden horizons, allowing each and everyone to live new experiences and see beyond his or her own particular world."(WEMF, 2005) According to Yahya R. Kamalipour, "In the midst of globalization and information explosion, communication plays a crucial role at all levels of human interaction, including interpersonal, organizational, regional, national, and international."(Kamalipour 2005)

Moreover, convergence and global media have "the potential to facilitate constructive dialogue, enhance viewers' knowledge and awareness, and bridge cultural and political gaps within" the Middle Eastern countries. (Kamalipour, 2005) Reuel Howe has pointed out that "communication means life or death to persons. Both the individual and society derive their basic meanings from the relations that exist between them. It is through dialogue that [humans] accomplish the miracle of personhood and community." (Kamalipour, 2005 & Howe, 1975) Governments and media moguls such as Prince Al-Waleed bin Talal, the Saudi businessperson, and others, politically and financially, support the information revolution, new communication technologies, and regional and global media. Anderson and Eickelman pointed out how "the Middle East features more of everything: media, especially transnational media, information, and erosion of boundaries to communication carefully erected by state monopolies."

Conclusion and Summary

Despite the realities of political, technical, cultural, and social challenges, media and communication convergence has gained wider participation in the Middle East. Convergence is alive and has bypassed the efforts of nearly all governments of the region to control the print and broadcast media. In addition, this chapter has focused on the internal and external challenges that Middle Eastern media organizations have been dealing with in the face of a rising media and business convergence. It also examined the structural development in the region and demonstrates the level of creativity the media mangers appeared to enjoy. This chapter has discussed the degree of influence global media have on local communication systems and media policies A predictable balance between utilizing new communication technology, acquiring highly qualified employees, and living up to the promises of delivering better content and media service were covered. Especially impressive are the increasing financial returns and the creation of a productive and encouraging working environment. Governmental and private media organizations have succeeded in positioning their organizations in competing with regional and global media. They provide extensive news coverage, drama, film, sports, and all kinds of entertainment programs - with much more variety to come.

References and Notes

Anderson, Jon W. and Eickelman, Dale F.(1999): *Media Convergence and Its Consequences.* Middle East Insight XIV(2): 59-61, March-April." Also check: http://www.georgetown.edu/research/arabtech/converges.htm.
Center for Contemporary Arab Studies:
http://aipnew.wordpress.com/2008/09/07/arab-information-project-specialist-workshops-1996/

Eickelman, Dale F. and Anderson, Jon W.(2003): New Media in the Muslim World: The Emerging Public Sphere:2ⁿᵈ Edition, Bloomington and Indianapolis :Indiana University Press.

Ilmarinen, Jussi(2005): Convergence soon brings added value for end users in the Middle East by AME Info FZ LLC in www.ameinfo.com
http://www.ameinfo.com/cgibin/cms/page.cgi?page=print;link=69583.

Henry, Clement M. and Springborg, Robert(2001): Globalization and the Politics of Development in the Middle East: (Cambridge, UK):Cambridge University Press.

Howe, Reuel L. (1975). The miracle of dialogue. Minneapolis, MN: Winston Press.
http://www.Al-bab.com/

Kamalipour Yahya R. (2005) The Battle of the Airwaves: The Rise and Proliferation of Iranian Satellite TV Channels Also check⊗TBS, 15) in http://www.tbsjournal.com/Kamalipour.html

Neher, W. William.(2003)(Development Communication in Africa, Concepts and Case Studies in Kwadwo Anokwa, el, International Communication: Thomson Wadsworth: United States 2003.

Palmer, Allen(2007), Following the Historical Paths of Global Communication, in Yahya R. Kamalipour, Global Communication(2007), 2ⁿᵈ ed.,: Australia and United States: Thomson, Wadsworth. P.17

Rhinesmith, Stephen(1996) A Manager's Guide to Globalization: Six Skills for Success in a Changing World. Chicago: Irwin Professional Publishing.

Rochlin, G. I. (1997). Trapped in the Net: The Unintended consequences of Computerization. Princeton, NJ: Princeton University Press.

Salamandra ,Christa.(2003). London's Arab Media and the Construction of Arabness. http://www.tbsjournal.com/Archives/Spring03/salamandra.html

Salsberg, B. (2003, September). Some advice for Journalism Students. Communicator, 10-12.

Simile; Aug 2005, Vol. 5 Issue 3. "The Arab Information Project Specialists Workshops: Jon Anderson of Catholic University speaking on the expansion of the Internet in the Middle East and Evelyn Early, an anthropologist with the US Information Agency, talking about the role of radio and television in Arab society.
http://www.georgetown.edu/research/arabtech/workshop.htm

Tanner, Andrea and Duhé, Sonya· Trends in Mass Media Education in the Age of Media Convergence: Preparing students for careers in a converging news environment.

Whitaker, Brian. http://www.al-bab.com/arab/about.htm.

World Electronic Media Forum: World Summit on the Information Society Broadcasters' Declaration; Tunis 15-17 November 2005.
http://aipnew.wordpress.com

www.http://www.nytimes.com/2009/06/16/world/middleeast/16media.html

Chapter Eight

The Demise of Traditional Legal Justifications for Broadcast Regulation

Steven Phipps
Maryville University

The American theory and practice of regulating broadcasting in contradistinction to the print media has been traditionally based on a hodge-podge of several legal justifications that supposedly naturally flow from the unique technological nature of broadcasting. Instead, however, legal rationale for broadcast regulation has been largely based on a myth, a myth that asserts that broadcasting possesses some sort of unique technological characteristics that, in turn, dictate the nature of regulation.

The problem with that view is that as broadcasting technology and various industry factors have changed, these traditional justifications have lost their efficacy. The real reasons for broadcast regulation, however, have never really been technology-driven. Although technological considerations have often been cited as the reason for regulating the broadcast media, the real reasons have concerned social goals and financial interests.

Practice of Regulating Broadcasting

Regulators would be fighting a losing battle if they were to attempt to construct new justifications today that are technology-based. Instead, any future rationale for the regulation of broadcasting must take into account societal and business needs, which have always served as the true underpinnings of the American system of broadcast regulation anyway.

In this chapter, we will first demonstrate inherent flaws in the scarcity of channels myth and related regulatory concepts. We will then consider the most likely future scenario for the regulation of the broadcast media in the United States.

The scarcity of channels

Over the decades since broadcasting began as a viable commercial medium in the early 1920s, one of the most prominent rationales for regulation has been based on the concept known as the scarcity of channels. In fact, this view has generally been advanced as the primary legal justification for regulation of American broadcast media in contradistinction to the print media.

The scarcity doctrine posits the view that the number of broadcast frequencies is finite and therefore the number of users must be limited. In other words, the number of available broadcast frequencies cannot possibly support the number of individuals wishing to broadcast. As a result, broadcasting is regulated by a federal agency acting as trustee for airwaves that are deemed public property.

Broadcast regulation has also been justified on the basis of the Constitution's Commerce Clause, which gives Congress authority over interstate commerce. The courts recognized in the 1920s that the only way to regulate broadcasting would be to regulate the industry as a whole. While some stations are intrastate, rather than interstate, in nature, the system of broadcasting in general was viewed as constituting interstate commerce.

This means that broadcasting, from a legal perspective, has been seen as constituting a very unique form of interstate commerce. According to that perspective, although broadcasting involves private business, the prevailing factors involved have to do with, again, the "public" airwaves.

Broadcasting, in other words, was deemed to involve private business that uses the public airwaves, airwaves that can only accommodate a limited number of stations engaged in private business. In that way, the concept of broadcasting as constituting interstate commerce has traditionally been intrinsically intertwined with the scarcity of channels concept.

After formation of the Federal Radio Commission (FRC), the first federal agency designed to exercise jurisdiction over broadcasting, the American court system determined through a series of court cases that events of the 1920s had proven that without limiting the number of broadcasters, "chaos" on the airwaves would result. This so-called "chaos" was usually viewed as the direct result of an overabundance of stations.

In actuality, however, events of the 1920s never did prove that the electromagnetic spectrum could not support the number of persons wishing to broadcast. That is because although broadcast "chaos" (i.e. interference) was blamed on a superabundance of stations, this was never demonstrated to be a sensible assessment of broadcasting at the time.

Other causes of interference were all but completely ignored. In more recent times, the legal doctrine of the scarcity of channels has been pushed aside in favor of other rationalizations for broadcast regulation. This has occurred as technological and regulatory changes are no longer clearly predicated on the concept of channel scarcity.

The emergence of broadcast regulation with the formation of the FRC in 1927 has never flowed out of necessity from some unique set of technological characteristics of the medium. Rather, certain technological characteristics, as defined at the time, were chosen as a basis for articulating a justification for requiring that broadcast stations be licensed but not newspapers.

Those technological characteristics were not, in other words, the reason for broadcast regulation; instead they were convenient excuses. The reason for broadcast regulation has never been the scarcity of channels; instead, the concept of the scarcity of channels was touted as a justification for regulation, while that regulation was actually based on considerations that had nothing to do with technology.

Further, those considerations had nothing to do with spectrum scarcity, but had everything to do with rationalizing the fledgling broadcast industry and ensuring profitability for the primary corporate players in broadcasting. Part of that process involved, as a side issue, the elimination of blatant abuses in terms of broadcast content.

Progressive Movement Model

By following the dominant Progressive Movement model of the era and bringing more stringent regulation to bear on the fledgling industry, small-time "Mom and Pop" operations in broadcasting were, for the most part, thrown out of the picture. At the same time, however, larger corporate industries were allowed to operate with higher power; to duplicate the same programming simultaneously on a number of stations via "chain" (network) broadcasting; and to gain wide coverage at night by use of AM "clear channels," the very existence of which precluded the operation of scores of local radio stations.

Today, while even the Federal Communications Commission openly advocates abandonment of the scarcity of channels concept (Berresford, 2005), the court system has been struggling to find new rationalizations for regulation of the broadcast industry. Those new rationalizations are not based on the technology of broadcasting as much as on the same two oftentimes unarticulated goals that guided the FRC - the Federal Radio Commission - as it assumed its regulatory posture beginning in 1927.

Those goals were and are to (1) rationalize the industry, ensuring profitability for major corporate players, and to (2) prevent blatant abuses in terms of programming content. The latter concern has given rise to an often-cited relatively new rationale for broadcast regulation: the pervasiveness doctrine.

As far as the scarcity of channels concept is concerned, however, a variety of factors that arose in broadcasting from the 1980s to the present have demonstrated that the concept should be regarded as suspect, at best. In fact, as already noted, the Federal Communications Commission (FCC) has itself abandoned the concept as a rationale for broadcast regulation.

In a white paper (Berresford, 2005), the Commission has noted that scarcity of channels is, in turn, based on the philosophy that the airwaves are public property. That paper suggests that this philosophy, a concept first articulated in the 1920s, never had any legal or technological basis. There is no deed by which the airwaves were ever made public property.

In addition, using the Commerce Clause as a justification for broadcast regulation in conjunction with the scarcity of channels concept poses a unique problem when the explosive growth in the importance of national newspapers in the last few decades is examined.

Are such national newspapers (or newspapers with national distribution) as *USA Today*, the *Wall Street Journal*, or the *New York Times* not engaged in interstate commerce? And, as various critics have been asking for decades ever since the number of competing daily papers started noticeably diminishing, are newspapers really immune to the scarcity of channels?

Reasons for "Chaos" in 1920s Broadcasting

Prior to passage of the Radio Act of 1927, which created the Federal Radio Commission (FRC), the primary authority for what little regulation then existed was vested in the Commerce Department and its chair, Herbert Hoover. One word then dominated discussion of the radio industry's pre-FRC problems: "chaos."

Commerce Department documents, the trade press, and the newspapers of the day frequently pointed to what was commonly termed "chaos on the airwaves," which was presented as an intolerable problem. "Chaos" was a synonym for interference. As listeners tuned in to their favorite radio stations, all too often "chaos" was said to be the result.

Actually, there was always some question as to the extent to which such interference even existed. Certainly there was some interference, but while some complained, others saw no major problem (Phipps, 2001, p. 59).

When the matter of interference were addressed by Hoover and industry representatives, only one proposed cause received any actual consideration, that being a supposed overabundance of stations. As a result, once the FRC's commissioners took office, their first major task became what was then termed the "weeding out" of stations.

Whether there was an overabundance of stations or not, enough other factors hindered the new broadcasting, industry that "chaos" would have characterized radio regardless. For one thing, the "DX" hobby, which focused on seeing how many distant stations one could pick up, was phenomenally popular.

Countless Americans attempted to listen to faint signals from far-away states and even other countries, noting their reception in special log books or charts widely distributed for that purpose. Certainly, this gave rise to extensive "interference" that might not have resulted had the same individuals been content to listen to much clearer local stations instead.

In addition, many radio receivers inadvertently transmitted, sending out interference to hinder reception on everyone else's radio in the same neighborhood. Commonly, 1920s radios - often using two knobs for tuning, not just one - were designed in such a way as to make tuning a difficult art to master.

Various other sources of radio interference remained in use during the '20s, unhindered by any government regulators. Antiquated transmitting equipment that interfered over wide geographical areas and over a number of frequencies simultaneously was still used by the military. Various types of newly-developed electrical devices - including X-ray machines and certain types of lighting devices - caused widespread radio interference, while nothing was being done to halt the problem.

Although the AM band was later extended from its original 535 to 1605 kiloHertz to 535-1705, during the 1920s the FRC insisted that the band could not be extended. Commercial broadcasters in the United States were already making limited experimental use of shortwave radio, but use of shortwave for expansion of domestic broadcasting services was never seriously discussed (Phipps, 1991a; Phipps, 2001).

Clearly, more frequencies could have been opened up for broadcasting, and a number of interference sources could have been eliminated. Still, only one factor was on the public and regulatory agenda during the 1920s: a supposed overabundance of stations. This highly questionable view resulted in the formulation of the legal doctrine of the scarcity of channels.

Establishment of the Legal Doctrine of the Scarcity of Channels

That doctrine was well codified by the time of the Red Lion case, Red Lion Broadcasting Co. v. FCC (1969). In that case, the Supreme Court quoted a Senate report from ten years earlier as claiming that "broadcast frequencies are limited and, therefore, they have been necessarily considered a public trust." The report then went to refer to those licensees who are "fortunate in obtaining a license" (Red Lion, 1969, p. 383).

The same concept was delineated, but certainly not first introduced, in the 1943 NBC case, National Broadcasting Co. v. U.S. Various sources have claimed or suggested that the scarcity of channels concept was first formulated in the NBC case (see, for example, Trauth, 1979, pp. 2-3; Gordon, 2006), but this is simply not true.

In NBC, the Supreme Court assessed the nature of broadcasting in the following terms:

> its facilities are limited; they are not available to all who may wish to use them; the radio spectrum simply is not large enough to accommodate

everybody. There is a fixed natural limitation upon the number of stations that can operate without interfering with one another (p. 213).

The scarcity doctrine had already been alluded to, however, in even earlier court cases involving broadcasting. In fact, the concept formed the basis for regulatory policy implemented by the Federal Radio Commission beginning in 1927. As an example of early application of the doctrine in the legal sphere, a federal district court in the 1929 case of U.S. v. American Bond & Mortgage Co. referred to what was seen as "the necessary limitation upon the number of stations" (p. 455).

In American Bond & Mortgage, the court suggested that by limiting the number of stations, the FRC was simply following precedent established by earlier court cases. In those cases, it was found justifiable to limit the number of slaughterhouses, banks, bars or taverns, and aircraft pilots (p. 456). The court further noted,

> Any kind of regulation in a limited field necessarily includes the possibility that some may be excluded from the field. Unregulated broadcasting would create a national nuisance, and the power of Congress extends to the adoption of all measures reasonably necessary for its prevention (p. 456).

In another case the following year, FRC officials came to St. Louis in order to force pirate radio operator George W. Fellowes off the air. The local judge trying the case remarked that the relatively new radio regulation was needed in order to, as he put it, "stop every Tom, Dick, and Harry from getting on the air" (Year for Radio, 1930, cited in Phipps, 1991b).

The notion of spectrum scarcity was directly upheld as a valid legal concept as recently as 1988, in the case known as U.S. v. Weiner (1988). In that case, broadcast frequencies were referred to as "scarce resource."

Allan Weiner had operated an unlicensed radio station called Radio New York International from a ship anchored past what he believed to be the limits of

U.S. territorial waters. He argued in vain that "radio should be as free and uncensored as the print media" ("Raiding," 1987, cited in Phipps, 1990).

Microbroadcasting and LPFM

With the 1970s and '80s came a widespread pirate radio movement in the United States (Phipps, 1990; Boyd, 1983, p. 203; Jones, 1994). Many pirate stations have operated only sporadically, for perhaps just a few minutes or an hour or two at a time, and likely with very low power. Their numbers, however, increased until the FCC found itself faced with a major "microbroadcasting" movement by the 1990s (Adams, 2004; Bishop, 2007; Coopman, 1999).

One of the most prominent microbroadcasters was Stephen Dunifer (U.S. v. Dunifer, 2000), who operated a radio station from his backpack while hiking in the hills above Berkeley, California. Dunifer insisted that the FCC's rationale for the present system of broadcast regulation, the scarcity of channels concept, was no longer tenable.

For a time, a federal district court agreed (Aguilar, 1999, pp. 1153-1154). Dunifer offered some cogent claims that the FCC's regulatory stance was content-based and served to meet the financial needs of corporate interests, instead of being based on technological characteristics of the medium (U.S. v. Dunifer, Order, 1998).

Microbroadcasters are so termed because they operate with very low power, oftentimes less than a watt. The very presence of this movement tended to demonstrate that the airwaves really could support more broadcasters than just those who were licensed, and without significant (if any) problems of interference. This fact, of course, served to further erode any remaining confidence in the soundness of the scarcity of channels concept.

As a matter of fact, the microbroadcasting movement appears to have been a primary reason behind the FCC's establishment in recent years of a legal low-power FM (LPFM) service (Adams, 2004; FCC Continues, 1998). In the 1990s, the National Association of Broadcasters (NAB), which is the country's leading trade association for the commercial broadcasting industry, became alarmed because of the potential for competition from microbroadcasters.

The NAB wanted the FCC to silence these unlicensed broadcasters. Generally, the FCC has bent a much-more-than-sympathetic ear toward NAB requests. In this case, however, the LPFM proposal was eventually forged through the regulatory channels, despite NAB objections.

At the same time that the FCC was considering LPFM, the Commission was receiving tens of thousands of inquiries about low-power broadcasting. Microbroadcasters converged on Washington in 1998, urging the FCC to consider a legal LPFM service.

Despite earnest protests on the part of the NAB, the FCC authorized LPFM in 2000. This enabled over 800 new low power stations to come on the air, without threatening the existence of higher-powered stations (Blofson, 2008).

Recent engineering studies have suggested that the airwaves could accommodate far more LPFM stations without interference. As a result, Congress is now considering directing the FCC to greatly expand the LPFM service, and all this in an industry supposedly dominated by a "scarcity of channels" (Blofson, 2008; FCC to LPFM). This demonstrates that the real concern behind pirate radio and microbroadcasting has not been that of interference, but rather of profitability for the major commercial players in the industry.

Technological Change Means that Channels are No Longer Scarce

A closely related issue is that, of course, technological changes in telecommunications have resulted in communication channels in general becoming anything but scarce. No longer are broadcasters limited to use of an archaic and technologically inefficient system which depends on using substantial electrical power to send out original programming on a one-time basis to a limited geographical area.

Now broadcasters can give the public on-demand programming - what they want, when they want it - through currently evolving Internet delivery systems supplemented by satellite radio. Those systems perhaps will offer the potential, after legal wrangling is resolved, to allow users to record programming for use later.

Even where broadcasting still operates in its traditional form, a growing tendency toward convergence means that it makes increasingly less sense to separate broadcasting from other media as particularly subject to regulation.

The emerging field of "convergence journalism," for example, often results in the production of media programming and content for more than one medium simultaneously. A single journalist might construct a given news story for use on a TV station, on a radio station, in a newspaper, and on the Internet.

The presence of this factor alone suggests that justification for regulation should shift from concern about technological characteristics of broadcast media to concern about ownership and content. The Supreme Court has not wanted to apply broadcast regulation principles to the Internet (Shapiro, p. 2), and the scarcity concept has never been applied in a regulatory sense to newspapers, outside of JOA (Joint Operating Agreement) provisions. The obvious question then becomes, should it continue to be applied to broadcasting?

Similarly, a federal appeals court noted in 1997 that direct broadcast satellite (DBS) is "not subject to anything remotely approaching the 'scarcity' that the Court found in conventional broadcast[ing] in 1969" in the Red Lion case and used in order to "justify a peculiarly relaxed First Amendment regime for such broadcast[ing]."

As Stephen Shapiro (1999, p. 7) noted in examining the gradual undermining of the scarcity of channels doctrine, "It would appear . . . that for all intents and purposes, the spectrum scarcity rationale is dead." In a study of the switch from analog to digital forms of telecommunication, Josephine Soriano (2006) has suggested that digital forms will bypass use of the electromagnetic spectrum entirely, while simultaneously opening up far more channels.

Scarcity of Channels Gives Way to the Pervasiveness Doctrine

From the beginning, the assumptions behind the legal doctrine known as the scarcity of channels (i.e. that "chaos" would result if the number of potential broadcasters was not limited, since there were more would-be broadcasters than available frequencies) were never proven. That doctrine was based on one historical interpretation of the pre-FRC state of affairs in broadcasting, as though current events that seemed to support that interpretation would remain frozen in time throughout future decades.

In the 1920s, newspapers were highly profitable and startup costs were still relatively low. By the 1970s and 1980s, many newspapers were suffering severely from an economic scarcity of channels. The Justice Department authorized Joint Operating Agreements (JOAs) designed to preserve what remained of the country's competing metropolitan dailies. By this time, clearly any scarcity doctrine seemed more applicable to the print media than to broadcasting.

In other words, competing dailies have been seen as sufficiently scarce as to justify JOAs, thereby, at least in theory, maximizing plurality of voices in the print media. At the same time, however, the FCC has abandoned the concept that ownership of broadcast properties must be limited in order to maximize plurality of voices in the broadcast media, the very media that were said to be using the "scarce" public airwaves. Not only are divergent voices being minimized, but Robert McChesney (2003) also points out that profits from broadcasting are being concentrated in fewer hands.

As already noted, because the legal doctrine known as the scarcity of channels no longer seems tenable as the primary justification for the regulation of broadcasting, courts have latched onto a relatively new doctrine that has been formulated in order to address an issue which remains of chief concern. The concern is that unwilling individuals are protected from having sleaze and violence thrust upon them through the broadcast media. The legal doctrine designed to prevent this from happening is known as the pervasiveness doctrine.

The pervasiveness doctrine suggests that, because of broadcasting's "pervasive" nature, its program content is difficult to escape. This is a concept that the Supreme Court first articulated (Wallace, 1998) in 1978 in the well-known case of FCC v. Pacifica Foundation. While driving with his son one afternoon and listening to a Pacifica station in New York, a man was shocked to hear comedian George Carlin recite the seven words that, as Carlin put it, you could not say on television.

The FCC and the court system then examined the concept of an individual's right to not hear or view undesired media content. While a need to protect children was recognized in the Pacifica case, the outcome of the case eventually led to a concern for adults' right to hear or view media content that is indecent (Glasser, 1980).

Obscene programming is prohibited by federal statute and is regarded by the Supreme Court as not protected speech. Concern, however, over adults' personal freedom to access indecent content (as contrasted with obscenity) resulted in the formulation of the Safe Harbor. The Safe Harbor is a time - currently midnight to 6 a.m. - when few children are presumed to be broadcast audience members, but when adults can freely tune in indecent programming.

In upholding the FCC's ability to protect children from such language during times when children can reasonably be expected to be in the audience in large numbers, the Supreme Court introduced the pervasiveness doctrine. Up to this point, the scarcity of channels had always been touted as sufficient rationale for broadcast regulation. Now, however, and much to the consternation of many who have been attempting to pin down the nature of broadcast regulation, the Court was introducing an entirely new legal doctrine.

As the industry has evolved, however, the pervasiveness doctrine has come to be seen as far more efficacious in a legal sense than the antiquated concept known as the scarcity of channels, a concept that has in recent years become shot full of holes.

Later court battles have considered, but not completely answered, the question of whether pervasiveness should apply to cable TV as well as broadcast TV. If a child is confronted by pornography on television, does it really matter whether it comes into the home via cable or by means of broadcast television?

On the other hand, the Supreme Court claimed in the 1997 decision of ACLU v. Reno that the Internet is not pervasive. The Internet, as the Court expressed it, is "not as invasive as radio or television." If the Internet is not invasive, then is television invasive, especially it television is eventually commonly delivered into the home via the Internet?

Now some are suggesting that even "pervasiveness" as a rationale for regulation is outmoded (e.g. Thierer, 2007). Rather than an overabundance of applicants for broadcast licenses, we are perhaps faced with an overabundance of means of communication. The number of media is increasing exponentially, and will any one of them emerge as any more "pervasive" than any of the others?

Creation of the pervasiveness doctrine, if actively pursued by the courts, could eventually release a Pandora's box of problems. If radio and television are pervasive, what else might be considered pervasive?

With all the channel choices and television options that currently exist regionally and globally, is television any more pervasive than a magazine or newspaper? Perhaps it could be argued that the mere presence of the pervasiveness doctrine serves to demonstrate that there is nothing clearly inherent about broadcasting that justifies its regulation in contradistinction to the print media.

Conclusion and Summary

Demand for regulation of the broadcast media has flowed not from the media's unique technological characteristics, but rather from concerns about profitability as well as concerns about potential negative effects from its programming. In other words, there never has been some inherent technological quirk of the broadcast media as compared to the print media - neither spectrum scarcity nor anything else - that has mandated that broadcasting be regulated as it has been since 1927.

As a result, any future legal rationale for broadcast regulation should consider social and economic goals, and any claims to supposed technological constraints that mandate that regulation take a certain form should be utterly abandoned. In formulating legal justifications for broadcast regulation in the future, the basic question to be asked should have nothing to do with broadcasting's technological characteristics, but rather the societal and economic goals sought by regulatory efforts.

References and Notes

Adams, Michael H., and Phipps, Steven, "Low-Power Radio/Microradio: Small Community Radio Stations," in Christopher H. Sterling, ed., *Encyclopedia of Radio*, Vol. 2, New York: Fitzroy Dearborn, 2004, pp. 885-887.

Aguilar, Michael J., "Micro Radio: A Small Step in the Return to Localism, Diversity, and Competitiveness in Broadcasting," *Brooklyn Law Review*, Vol. 65, Winter 1999, pp. 1133-?.

Berresford, John W., *The Scarcity Rationale for Regulating Traditional Broadcasting: An Idea Whose Time Has Passed*, Federal Communications Commission Media Bureau Staff Research Paper No. 2005-2, 2005.

Bishop, Ed, "Review - Funny, Informative Doc Looks at Relationship of Radio, FCC," *St. Louis Journalism Review*, July 2007, pp. 10, 26.

Blofson, Kate, "LFFM's Rallying Cry - Low Power to the People! The Prometheus Radio Project Raises the Barn for Community Access," *Popular Communications*, March 2008, pp. 15-18.

Boyd, Douglas A., "Radio Free America: The U.S. Government's Reaction to Pirate Radio," *Central States Speech Journal*, Vol. 34, Fall 1983, pp. 203-209.

Coopman, Ted M., "FCC Enforcement Difficulties with Unlicensed Micro Radio," *Journal of Broadcasting & Electronic Media*, Vol. 43, No. 4, Fall 1999, pp. 582-602.

"FCC Continues Crackdown on 'Pirate' Radio Broadcasters," *The News Media & the Law*, Fall 1998, p. unknown.

"FCC to LPFM Community: The More the Merrier," *Monitoring Times*, January 2008, p. 6.

Glasser, Theodore L., and Harvey C. Jassem, "The Right Not to Hear as a Rationale for Broadcast Regulation: A Review and an Appraisal," ERIC Document number ED198582, 1980.

Gordon, Joshua B., "Pacifica is Dead, Long Live Pacifica: Formulating a New Argument Structure to Preserve Government Regulation of Indecent Broadcasts," *Southern California Law Review*, Vol. 79, September 2006, pp. 1451-?.

Jones, Steve, "Unlicensed Broadcasting: Content and Conformity," *Journalism Quarterly*, Vol. 71, No. 2, Summer, 1994, pp. 395-402.

McChesney, Robert M., "The FCC's Big Grab: Making Media Monopoly Part of the Constitution," *Counterpunch*, May 16, 2003, no pagination.

National Broadcasting Company v. U.S., 319 U.S. 190 (1943).

Phipps, Steven, "The Commercial Development of Short Wave Radio in the United States, 1920-1926," *Historical Journal of Film, Radio, and Television*, Vol. 11, No. 3, 1991, pp. 215-227 (Phipps, 1991a).

Phipps, Steven, "'Order Out of Chaos:' A Reexamination of the Historical Basis for the Scarcity of Channels Concept," *Journal of Broadcasting & Electronic Media*, Vol. 45, No. 1, 2001, pp. 57_74.

Phipps, Steven, "Unlicensed Broadcasting and the Federal Radio Commission: The 1930 George W. Fellowes Challenge," *Journalism Quarterly*, Vol. 68, No. 4, 1991, pp. 823-828 (Phipps, 1991b).

Phipps, Steven, "Unlicensed Broadcasting in the U.S.: The Official Policy of the FCC," *Journal of Broadcasting & Electronic Media*, Vol. 34, No. 2, 1990, pp. 137-152.

"Raiding the Radio Pirates of New York," *Newsweek*, August 10, 1987, p. 21.

Red Lion Broadcasting Co., Inc. v. Federal Communications Commission, 395 U.S. 367.

Shapiro, Stephen J., "One and the Same: How Internet Non-Regulation Undermines the Rationales Used to Support Broadcast Regulation," *Media Law & Policy*, Vol. 8, Fall 1999, pp. 1-?.

Soriano, Josephine, "Note: The Digital Transition and the First Amendment: Is it Time to Reevaluate Red Lion's Scarcity Rationale?" *Boston University Public Interest Law Journal*, Vol. 15, Spring 2006, pp. 341-356.

Thierer, Adam, "Why Regulate Broadcasting? Toward a Consistent First Amendment Standard for the Information Age," *Journal of Communications Law & Policy*, Vol. 15, 2007, pp. 431-482.

Time Warner Entertainment Co. v. Federal Communications Commission, On Suggestions for Rehearing *In Banc*, U.S. Court of Appeals for the District of Columbia Circuit, Februarty 7, 1997, Document No. 93-5349.

Trauth, Denise M., and John L. Huffman, "The Pacifica Case: The Supreme Court's New Regulatory Rationale for Broadcasting," ERIC Document No. ED 184 149, 1979.

U.S. v. American Bond & Mortage Co., 31 F.2d 448 (1929).

U.S. v. Dunifer, 997 F.Supp. 1235 (1998).

U.S. v. Dunifer, 219 F.3d 1004 (2000).

U.S. v. Dunifer, Order Granting Plantiff's Motion for Summary Judgment and Granting Permanent Injunction, U.S. District Court, N.D. California, FCC Document No. C 94-03542 CW (year?).

U.S. v. Weiner, 701 F.Supp. 14 (1988).

Wallace, Jonathan D., "Supreme Court's Rulings Threaten Free Speech," *USA Today*, March 1999 (exact date and page number unknown).

"Year for Radio Outlaw; Paroled for Deportation," *St. Louis Post-Dispatch*, May 10, 1930, p. 1A.

Chapter Nine

Conclusion and Outlook

Jabbar A. Al-Obaidi &
William G. Covington, Jr.

Global media and communication technology is one of the highlights of two conventions which usually take place in Las Vegas, Nevada, USA, the annual conventions of the National Association of Broadcasters and the Broadcast Education Association. A central concern at these conventions has been how media content and delivery systems are significantly impacted by recent technological development to the point where media and communication managements have started to look for new creative ways to stay in business and to remain competitive.

Most of the chapters in this book have grown from work initially presented at the BEA convention. We came up with the idea of collaborating on this project to track the development of media technology and the use of new social media in different institutions at a university level. Such discussion necessarily involves the four main components in typical communication settings: a receiver, a medium, a message, and a feedback. As well, each of the contributors offered a unique niche in which he or she had expertise. A key strength in the work is the international perspective that extends the vista of the emerging media landscape into a multicultural dimension. Timeliness is another element in the mix that should be taken into account. Although a book, by nature, is a snapshot of change as it occurs, there are some constants to be found as well.

While media and communication managements are seeking new directions for their producers and programmers that would enable them to build a relevant formula in a complex international emerging media marketplace, marketplace in the context of this book is not limited to financial considerations, but primarily focuses on the marketplace of ideas and its evolution. Though regulatory considerations are being negotiated continually, the technology remains one-step ahead of the regulators. New delivery systems make old ways of regulating media obsolete. Popular culture increasingly becomes global in nature and sadly, some local cultures are lost along the way.

This characterization is not to say that individuals in the emerging media culture are inert victims. The interactive nature of the emerging technologies allows users to be more active than passive. All forms of media allow for some form of activity, for example, in print media, a reader has to make a choice of reading material, determine the amount of time he or she will be reading, and turn a page. However, the new technologies magnify this active component many times over. Apparently, "Reading" a webpage presents a variety of choices. There are links to choose from, scanning to be considered, a determination on how much will be read or which icons will be selected to move to another page. The process is designed to attract more people, and consequently it is oriented toward them as strategic users and not as subjects of the producer.

Producers in the interactive media have to be more creative to compete effectively in an environment with more options. Incorporating verbocentric (traditionally written) texts with artwork, logos, and other symbol systems makes the creation of a media product more complicated. However, user-friendly technology makes the process easier than ever for people who might feel technically incompetent. With more products created, the result can be information overload and a splintering of desires, personal preferences, and interest groups. Hence, co-cultures are created, sustained, and promoted. All is based on information access and preferences. Rather than geography, politics, or ideology being the determining factor, content becomes the feature around which individuals gather. Consequently, the sense of traditional place starts to lose its importance. Interestingly enough, the developing and even the less developed countries have decided to jump on the broadband wagon to catch up or at least to do something related to the expansion of global communication technology. These countries have the burning desire to beat the factors that seem to continue deterring convergence in the information technology market. In the word of Omar Kaaki, general manager of FastTelco: (The Report, Kuwait, 2009)

> *The primary factor is the lack of a regulator that governs this type of business here in Kuwait. To be more specific, there is no regulator to float licenses and handle bidding and usage. To put simply, the role of regulator has been left empty.*

Kaaki also brought up the issue of security in the area of global communication and developing corporate business management. He argued "the security of data is extremely important. This is the leading priority in information technology. We have developed many solutions in managed security services such as firewalls and other preventative measures." (The Report, 2009) In a fast changing era of technology convergence, fighting against software piracy, copyrights violation, and protection of intellectual property seem to take number one priority on the agenda of governments and the United Nations. Nations, organizations, and concerned citizens come together to enforce international regulations and conventions in order to safeguard their applications world wide.

New Digital Communication Technologies

The last decade (2000-2010) brought us new or more developed lines of communication that have been put to use by individuals, professionals, businesses, governments, organizations, and the media. The blog, the latest fad in digital communication technology has proven its worth to millions of people around the world. The phenomena of blogging became popular in the last decade. According to the Webster Dictionary, a blog is "a Web site that contains an online personal journal with reflections, comments, and often hyperlinks provided by the writer (http://www.merriam-webster.com/dictionary/blog). The word blog is short for weblog. The Encyclopedia Britannica has a longer more in depth definition. Blogs are an "online journal where an individual, group, or corporation presents a record of activities, thoughts, or beliefs. Some blogs operate mainly as news filters, collecting various online sources and adding short comments and Internet links. Other blogs concentrate on presenting original material. In addition, many blogs provide a forum to allow visitors to leave comments and interact with the publisher. 'To blog' is the act of composing material for a blog. Materials are largely written, but pictures, audio, and videos are important elements of many blogs. The 'blogosphere' is the online universe of blogs. Hence, blogs have become essential part of the information delivery system around the world."(http://www.britannica.com/EBchecked/topic/869092/blog) Blogs have been studied and findings revealed by studies, varied by demographics, but the studies gave some interesting conclusions. Haferkamp and Kramer (2008) found that women bloggers in particular used their blog for social networking purposes, which is also why they commented on other's blogs. In contrast, men bloggers were more motivated by self-publicity. However, schools' institutional blogs were more motivated by engaging students and advancing interactions between learners and teachers.

Micro blogs are a more recent modification, and whether you are teaching students, training technicians, working with politicians, attempting to jump start a local business, trying to broadcast your latest hit single, or simply attempting to share your day with your friends and family, you will find the newest development of a micro blogging platform extremely useful. One of the most noticeable technologies has been Twitter. Since its creation in March 2006, Twitter has grown into a billion dollar company (Liedtke), and all of it is based on the concept of answering one simple question: What are you doing? Twitter users keep a micro-blog of 140-character status updates about anything that the users want to say. Their tweets are posted to their own profile, and then are spread to the Twitter users' followers on home screens, as well as to any number of twitter-friendly applications that send updates to Twitter followers' internet homepages, cell phones, mobile internet devices, or other services. Tweets can also be directed at another user, by including @username, or can be charted and searched according to topic, if the topic name is marked with the symbol #. Google C.E.O. Eric Schmidt has described his feelings about Twitter, saying "Speaking as a computer scientist, I view all of these as sort of a poor man's email systems" (Frommer). Because of real-time updates facilitated by many choices of notification on a variety of technical devices, Twitter is a way for a user's opinions and thoughts to be heard instantly by a constantly growing number of followers, and that reach has caused many people to wonder about the effects of this new form of instant communication.

In the summer of 2009, on-line estimates suggest that Twitter was growing at 1,382 percent annually (Ostrow), and the total number of users was closing in on 6 million users, up from just slightly over 1 million the same time in 2008 (Ostrow). During that time period, the Hollywood release of new summer movies into theaters was impacted by micro blogs, and what happened has been named "The Twitter effect." Twitter users who went to an opening night or opening weekend showing of a movie would tweet their reactions to the film, and their followers received the user thoughts instantly. The tweet followers would base their decision on whether or not to see the movie themselves from these tweets.

This Twitter effect has been covered from both positive and negative lights. Ticket sales for the movie *Brüno*, for example, dropped 39% between opening Friday and Saturday (Van Grove), and some attribute the drop to unfavorable Twitter reviews and reactions to the film. The movie *Paranormal Activity*, on the other hand, was so widely praised and demanded in tweets, that it went from showing in 13 theaters to over a thousand, and becoming the most profitable movie ever made (Jacobson), grossing more than $107 million dollars to date (The numbers) with a production budget of only $15,000 (Jacobson).

The rate at which Twitter is growing and breaking into more of our online community is astounding. There is growing sense to the idea that something that can be read by over 5 million people is a powerful tool to spread ideas and opinions, as well as useless blurbs about what someone is eating for lunch right now. Businesses around the world use Twitter to advertise and advance new ideas to societies and cultures all around the world. This platform is a quick and easy way to get information out to the public and to ensure that the word will spread quickly.

Speaking of digital media and communication changes, Rupert Murdoch who is the president of News Corporation and one of the most powerful figures in the media industry said it best about the future of news media in this global era:

> *What is happening right before us is, in short, a revolution in the way young people are accessing news. They do not want to rely on the morning paper for their up-to-date information. They do not want to rely on a godlike figure from above to tell them what's important; they want their news on demand, when it works for them. They want control over their media, instead of being controlled by it. They want to question, to probe, to offer a different angle.*

Humanistic Theory

Uses and gratifications theory looks at the media in a humanistic way. This formulation states that there is much more than just one way to use the media, that there are many ways of using the media just as there are many users of the media. According to the theory, media users have complete free will concerning how they will use the media and how the media may affect them. (Barton 14). Blumler and Katz believe that users control the influence media has on them. Many accept this analysis because each individual makes a choice at some level about what kind of media to which he or she is exposed. There are varied reasons why individuals choose different types of media, individual reasons based on particular uses that are offered and gratifications that are sought. This theory explains that the user employs the media as a means to an end. This use explains how people use Twitter, a means to an end. Although it is a simple micro blogging network, many people, businesses, and celebrities use it for specific benefit: profit, self-expression, dissemination of ideas, and social commentary to name a few. When they use Twitter as well as other forms of media, they are trying to fulfill needs that they have set for themselves whether consciously or not.

For another example, one can illustrate uses and gratification theory in terms of music selection along two lines. Frequently, individuals select a type of music to fit a particular mood or to change it. Such use reflects an individual's desire to affect his or her inner landscape for a specific need. Individuals also tend to listen to certain genres of music and artists because they are accepted in the social circles to which the individuals choose to belong. Such use reflects the individual's desire to affect his or her external social landscape, also to fit specific needs. These music selections, uses, are a form of media choice that an individual can make in order to fulfill personal needs for mood change and for a sense of social acceptance, gratifications. The importance of individual, personal choice and control can be argued in the uses and gratification formulation.

Clickable Pointers

An undeniable reality is that digital information technology has touched every corner of today's society. Colleges, universities, governmental institutions, and business organizations already have adopted new software to better handle data, registrations, grant applications, financial issues, academic, administrative, and organizational affairs. The United Nations, and other global organizations, and federal governments are still seeking new innovative ways to integrate online communication modules.

Truly, new media is changing the global landscape, not only in the United Sates and Europe but also in Asia, Africa, and the Middle East. A case in point, in November 2006 the Al-Jazeera network introduced its first devoted news channel on YouTube, with video news averaging 2m-5m views per month in early 2009. (The Report, Qatar, 2009) In January 2009, Al-Jazeera English news bulletins contracted with the British newspaper *The Independent* to use its website to broadcast Al-Jazeera English news. Moreover, Al-Jazeera launched its services on the social networking site Facebook. (The Report, Qatar, 2009) That network has offered Al-Jazeera video views via mobile phone to more than 1.8 million subscribers.

The Challenge of Filtering and Focusing

With global and converging media comes multitasking. Perhaps one of the most disturbing challenges in our lives is that in the era of digital media and technology our attention span has sharply declined. Henry Jenkins has alarmed us about this kind of transformation: (Jenkins, 2009)

All information to be processed by our brains is temporarily held in short-term memory, and the capacity of our short-term memory is sharply limited. Learners must filter out extraneous information and sharpen their focus on the most salient details of their environment.

With so much mediated and unmediated information available to every individual, the challenge about how to filter the overflow is daunting. On the individual rests squarely the burden.

In conclusion, there is no equivocation to the fact that global communication has converged and with its convergence has come a sea of changes and a flood of new trends in the way we deal with media and communication. The constant is that there seems to be no end to the dramatic and fast changing nature of communication technology. The ever-transforming digital age is a reality of the twenty-first century in which the world is connected by electronic networks. MySpace, Facebook, Tweeter, YouTube, and other social networking are here to stay with us as their forms, styles, and contents evolve. All can be accessed by clicking hyperlinks to get text, visuals, music and much more online information.

One caution needs to be kept in mind: media and technology literacy. People need to learn how to access, evaluate, interpret, and use information responsibly and with a great deal of transparency and accountability. Who gives that instruction is one key to the future.

References and Notes

Frommer, D. (2009, March 3). Google CEO: Twitter a *'poor man's email system'*. *Business Insider*, Retrieved from http://www.businessinsider.com/google-ceo-twitter-a-poor-mans-email-system-2009-3.
  Encyclopedia Britannica. 2009. Encyclopedia Britannica Online. 18 Feb 2009 http://www.britannica.com/EBchecked/topic/869092/blog.
Haferkamp, Nina, and Nicole Kramer. *"Entering the Blogosphere: Motives for Reading, Writing, and Commenting."* International Communication Association (2008). Communication & Mass Media Complete.
Jacobson, S. (2009, October 30). *Paranormal activity is most profitable film ever*. The First Post, Retrieved from http://www.thefirstpost.co.uk/55417,news-comment,entertainment,paranormal-activity-is-the-most-profitable-film-ever.
Liedtke, M. (2009, September 25). *Something to tweet about: twitter valued at $1b*. PhysOrg, Retrieved from http://www.physorg.com/news173108253.html Merriam-Webster Online Dictionary. 2009
Merriam-Webster Online. 18 February 2009. http://www.merriam-webster.com/dictionary/blog
Ostrow, A. (2009, April 6). *Twitter and Myspace post huge growth numbers in March*. Retrieved from http://mashable.com/2009/04/06/twitter-and-facebook-post-huge-growth-numbers-in-march/.
Ostrow, A. (2009, March 16). *Twitter now growing at staggering 1,382 percent*. Mashable, Retrieved from http://mashable.com/2009/03/16/twitter-growth-rate-versus-facebook/.
Van Grove, J. (2009, July 13). *Did opening night twitter reviews sink Bruno's weekend box office?*. Mashable Social Media Guide, Retrieved from http://mashable.com/2009/07/13/bruno-twitter-reactions/.
Van Grove, J. (2009, August 24). *Twitter effect redux: 78% of tweets about Inglorious Basterds were positive*. Mashable Social Media Guide, Retrieved from http://mashable.com/2009/08/24/inglourious-basterds-tweets/. (http://www.merriam-webster.com/dictionary/blog)
The Report, *Kuwait*. (2009). Oxford Business Group
The Report, *Qatar*, (2009). Oxford Business Group.

Bibliography

Adams, Michael H., and Phipps, Steven, "Low-Power Radio/Microradio: Small Community Radio Stations," in Christopher H. Sterling, ed., *Encyclopedia of Radio*, Vol. 2, New York: Fitzroy Dearborn.

Accrediting Council on Education in Journalism and Mass Communications (2001). *Journalism and Mass Communications Accreditation* 2007-2008.

Aguilar, Michael J., "Micro Radio: A Small Step in the Return to Localism, Diversity, and Competitiveness in Broadcasting," *Brooklyn Law Review*, Vol. 65, Winter 1999.

Ajemian, P. (2008, January 28). The Islamist opposition online in Egypt and Jordan. Retrieved June 14, 2008, from *Arab Media & Society*: http://www.arabmediasociety.com/?article=577

Allam, R. (2008, February 19). "Satellite TV Content Regulation: One Step Forward". Retrieved March 4, 2008, from *Daily News Egypt*: *http://www.dailystaregypt.com/article.aspx?ArticleID=11970*

Ambah, F. S. (2008, April 27). Saudi Activist Blogger Freed After 4 Months in Jail without Charge. Retrieved June 14, 2008, from *Washingtonpost.com: http://www.washingtonpost.com/wpdyn/content/article/2008/04/26/AR200 8042601470.html*

Anderson, B. (1991). *Imagined communities: Reflections of the origin and spread of nationalism* (2nd ed.). New York: Verso.

Anderson, Jon W. and Eickelman, Dale F.(1999): Media Convergence and Its Consequences. *Middle East Insight* XIV(2): 59-61, March-April." Also check: http://www.georgetown.edu/research/arabtech/converges.htm.

Anderson, K. (2007, November 28). YouTube suspends Egyptian blog activist's account. Retrieved June 14, 2008, from *NewsBlog: http://blogs.guardian.co.uk/news/2007/11/youtube_suspends_egyptian_bl og.html*

Annabelle, S.(2001). Mediated Culture in the Middle East: Diffusion, Democracy, Difficulties. *Gazette* Vol. 63(2-3) , 101- 119.

Arab Media: How Governments Handle the News". (2008, February 8).
Retrieved March 4, 2008, from *The Economist:*
http://www.economist.com/world/africa/displaystory.cfm?story_id=10666
436.Abou-Alsamh, R. (2006, June 19). Saudi women unveil opinions
online. Retrieved June 24, 2008, from *The Christian Science Monitor:*
http://www.csmonitor.com/2006/0619/p06s02- wome.html

Arab Networks for Human Rights (2008). Implacable Adversaries: Arab
Governments and the Internet. (n.d.). Retrieved June 15, 2008, *The*
Arab Network for Human Rights Information:
http://www.openarab.net/en/node/346

:(2006). Implacable Adversaries: Arab Governments and the Internet.
Retrieved March 2, 2008, from *The Arabic Network for Human Rights*
Information
http://www.openarab.net/en/reports/net2006/blogger.shtmlRinfo):

Arab States Broadcasting Union (2008). Description of the current
situation of Arab satellite channels,' at:
http://www.asbu.net/www/en/doc.asp?mcat=5&mrub=33.

Awad, A. (2005). Online journalism in the Arab world. *Proceedings of the*
conference on online journalism in the Arab world, University of Sharjah,
UAE, Nov. 5-6.

Ayish, M. (2001). American-style journalism and Arab World television: An
exploratory study of news selection at six Arab world satellite television
channels,' *Transnational Broadcasting Journal.* No. 6, Spring\summer at:
http://www.tbsjournal.com/Archives/Spring01/Ayish.html.
(2002). Political communication on Arab world television: Evolving
patterns. *Political Communication.* No. (19).

:(2008). *The new Arab public sphere.* Berlin: Frank & Timme.

Balcytiene, A. (2002). Lithuanian media—a question of change. In P. Vihalemm
(Ed.), Baltic media in transition (pp. 103-134). Tartu: Tartu University
Press.

Barber, B. (1984). *Strong Democracy: Participation Politics for the New Age.*
Berkeley: University of California Press.

Barlow, J. P. (1996, February 8). A Declaration of the Independence of
Cyberspace Retrieved June 10, 10, from

http://homes.eff.org/~barlow/Declaration-Final.html

Bell, D. (1973). The Coming of the Post Industrial Society. New York: Basic .

Berman, J., & Daniel, W. J. (1997). Technology and Democracy. *Social Research*, Vol. 64, No 3, Fall.

Berresford, John W., *The Scarcity Rationale for Regulating Traditional Broadcasting: An Idea Whose Time Has Passed*, Federal Communications Commission Media Bureau Staff Research Paper No. 2005-2, 2005.

Best, M. L., & Wade, K. W. (2005, October). The Internet and Democracy: Global Catalyst or Democratic Dud? Retrieved June 10, 2008, from *http://ssrn.com/abstract=870080*

Bird, E., Lutz, R. and Warick, C. (2008). Media as partners in education for sustainable development: A training and resource kit. *UNESCO* Series on Journalism Education. Paris: UNESCO Publishing.

Bishop, Ed, "Review - Funny, Informative Doc Looks at Relationship of Radio, FCC," *St. Louis Journalism Review*, July 2007.

Blofson, Kate, "LFFM's Rallying Cry - Low Power to the People! The Prometheus Radio Project Raises the Barn for Community Access," *Popular Communications*, March 2008, pp. 15-18.

Blogger Abdul Moneim Freed, But Kareem Amer Still Held. (2007, June 4). Retrieved June 14, 2008, from Reporters Without Borders: http://www.rsf.org/article.php3?id_article=21995

Bowers, J. (1993). *American Stories: Case Studies in Government and Politics*. Belmont, CA:Wadsworth Publishing Company.

Bowers, J. , Claflin, B. and Walker, G. (1998). A case study from Rochester, New York: The impact of civic journalism projects on voting behavior in state-wide referendums, a paper presented at the Annual Meeting of the New England Political Science Association, May 1-2, Worcester, MA.

Boyd, Douglas A., "Radio Free America: The U.S. Government's Reaction to Pirate Radio," *Central States Speech Journal*, Vol. 34, Fall 1983.

Brody, Jeffrey H. 2000. "The Structure of the Internet Industry," in A. N. Greco. *The Media and Entertainment Industries*. Boston: Allyn and Bacon.

Brooks, P. (1976). *The melodramatic imagination: Balzac, Henry James, melodrama, and the mode of excess*. Clinton: Colonial Press.

Browers, M. (2006). *Democracy and civil society in Arab political thought: Trans-cultural possibilities*. New York: Syracuse University Press.

Buckingham, Marcus. 2007. Go: *Put Your Strengths to Work*. New York: Free Press.

Campbell, R. (2003). Media and Culture: An introduction to mass communication. Boston: Bedford/St. Martin's Press.

Castells, M. (2008). The New Public Sphere: Global Civil Society, Communication Networks, and Global Governance. The ANNALS of the American Academy of Political and Social Science, 78-93.

Cecchini, M. (2003). Active citizenship, adult learning and active citizenship, lifelong learning and active citizenship, Key note speech.EAEA Conference, Nicosia, Cyprus, 15 November.

Center for Contemporary Arab Studies
http://aipnew.wordpress.com/2008/09/07/arab-information-project-specialist-workshops-1996/

Cogan, J. (1998). Citizenship education for the 21st century: Setting the context,' in Cogan, J. & Derricott, R. (eds), *Citizenship for the 21st century: An international perspective on education*, London, Kogan Page.

Colon, A. (2000). The multimedia newsroom. Columbia Journal Review. 24-27. Communication Networks, and Global Governance. The ANNALS of the American Academy of Political and Social Science, 78-93. communication. Boston: Bedford/St. Martin's Press.

Compton, M. (Spring 2008). One Newsroom Fits All. *Jargon* Vol. LXIX (Issue 1)

Coopman, Ted M., (1999) "FCC Enforcement Difficulties with Unlicensed Micro Radio," *Journal of Broadcasting & Electronic Media*, Vol. 43, No. 4, Fall 1999.

Courter, B. (March 19, 2008). Chattanooga State Radio Station Going Online; Tower, License To Be Sold. *Chattanooga Times Free Press*. Retrieved March 20, 2008 from http://chattan.com/articles/article_124219.asp.

: (March 28, 2008). Courter: Clearing the air regarding WAWL's sale. *Chattanooga Times Free Press*. Retrieved March 31, 2008 from http://timesfreepress.com/news/2008/mar/28/courter-clearing-air-regarding-wawls-sale/.

CPJ. (2007, November 27). Critical writer jailed in Tunisia. Retrieved June 14, 2008, From Committee to Protect Journalists CPJ News Alert:http://www.cpj.org/news/2007/mideast/tunisia26novt07na.html

Criado, C., & Krapelin, C. (2003). Convergence Journalism: Landmark U.S. media and university study. Convergence Journlaim.com

Curtin, M. (1996). On edge: Culture industries in the neo-network era. In A. Ohmann, G. Averill, M. Curtin, D. Shumway, & E. G. Traube (Eds.), Making and selling culture. Hanover: Wesleyan University Press.

Da Lage, O. (2005). The politics of Al Jazeera or the diplomacy of Doha, in Zayani, M. (ed.), *Al Jazeera phenomenon: Critical perspectives on new Arab media*. New York: Pluto Press.

Daniel, W. (2006). Lifelong learning of the future: A vision, a paper presented at the *Roundtable on Learning from the Past to Build the Future*, European Schoolnet, Burgess, Belgium, Dec. 7-8.

Denton, F. and Thorson, E. (1994). 'Civic journalism: Does it work? A special report for the Pew Center for Civic Journalism on the "We the People" project,' Madison, Wis.

De-Sola Pool, I. (1983). Technologies of Freedom. Cambridge, Mass: The Belknap Press of Harvard University Press.

Devereux, Edward C. Jr.(1961). "Parsons' Sociological Theory," In Max Black ed. The Social Theories of Talcott Parsons. Englewood Cliffs, NJ: Prentice-Hall, 1961.

Dubai Press Club. (2008). *Arab media outlook: 2008-2012*. London: Price Water House Coopers.

Dubrin, Andrew J. 2001. (1978). Human Relations: Interpersonal, Job-Oriented Skills 7th ed. Upper Saddle River, NJ: Prentice Hall.

EAO.(1994/95). Statistical Yearbook 1994/95. Strasbourg: European Audiovisual Observatory. (2004). Statistical Yearbook 2004 (2 volumes). Strasbourg: European Audiovisual Observatory.

Eggerton, John.(2008) "Are News Habits Really Changing?" Broadcasting & Cable. March 17, 2008.

Eickelman, Dale F. and Anderson, Jon W.(2003): New Media in the Muslim World: The Emerging Public Sphere:2nd Edition, Bloomington and Indianapolis :Indiana University Press.

El-Nawawi, M. and A. Iskander. (2003). *Al-Jazeera: How the free Arab news network scooped the world and changed the Middle East.* Cambridge, MA: Westview.

: (2002). AL-JAZEERA: *How the Free Arab News Network Scooped the World and Changed the Middle East.* Westview Press.

Encyclopedia Britannica. 2009. *Encyclopedia Britannica Online.* 18 Feb 2009 http://www.britannica.com/EBchecked/topic/869092/blog.

Fales, A. W. (1996). Lifespan learning development, 183-187. In Colin J.T. (ed.) *Lifelong education for adults: An international handbook.* Pergamon Press.

FCC (1998)Continues Crackdown on 'Pirate' Radio Broadcasters," *The News Media & the Law,* Fall 1998.

FCC to LPFM Community: (2008) The More the Merrier," *Monitoring Times,* January 2008.

Fam, M. (2008, May 5). Egyptian Political Dissent Unites Through Facebook: Activists Make Use of New Technology Across Arab World. Retrieved June 9, 2008, from *The Wall Street Journal: http://online.wsj.com/article/SB120975285862963213.html*

Fikr (Arab Thought Foundation). (2008). *Arab cultural development report.* Beirut: Fikr Publishing.

Flannigan, W. and Zingale, N. (1994). *Political behavior of the American electorate*. Washington, D.C.: CQ Press.

Fretwell, D. and Colombano, J. (2000). *Emerging policies and programs for the 21st century in upper and middle income countries*. Washington, D. C.: World Bank.

Friedland, L. (2002). Measuring civic journalism's progress: A report across a decade of activity, a study conducted for the Pew Center for Civic Journalism.

Friedman, L. Thomas (2005) *The World is Flat: A Brief History of the Twenty-First Century*. New York: Farrar, Straus &Giroux.

Frommer, D. (2009, March 3). Google CEO: Twitter a *'poor man's email system'*. *Business Insider*, Retrieved from http://www.businessinsider.com/google-ceo twitter-a-poor-mans-email-system-2009-3.

Gamson, J. (1998). *Freaks talk back: Tabloid talk shows and sexual nonconformity*. Chicago: University of Chicago Press.

Garton Ash, T. (1990). The magic lantern: *The revolution of '8 witnessed in Warsaw, Budapest, Berlin, and Prague*. New York: Random House.

Gilder, G. (1992). *Life after television: The coming transformation of television and the American Life*. New York: W.W. Norton & Company.

Glasser, Theodore L., and Harvey C. Jassem.(1980). "The Right Not to Hear as a Rationale for Broadcast Regulation: A Review and an Appraisal," ERIC Document number ED198582, 1980.

Gordon, Joshua B., (2006). "Pacifica is Dead, Long Live Pacifica: Formulating a New Argument Structure to Preserve Government Regulation of Indecent Broadcasts," *Southern California Law Review*, Vol. 79, September 2006.

Gordon, R. (2006). Convergence defined. USC Annenberg: *Online Journalism Review*.

Gow, J., Paterson, R., & Preston, A. (Eds.) (1996). *Bosnia by television*. London: British Film Institute.

Grei, J. Michael (2000). Globalisation. In Jureidini & Poole *"Sociology: Australian Connections (2nd Ed)"* Sydney:Allen & Unwin.

Haferkamp, Nina, and Nicole Kramer. *"Entering the Blogosphere: Motives for Reading, Writing, and Commenting."* International Communication
Association (2008). Communication & Mass Media Complete.

Hamdy, N. (2006). Alternative Arab Voices: A Depiction of the Usage of Blogs in Cyberspace. International Association for Media and Communication Research IAMCR. Cairo, Egypt.

Hamdy, N., & Mobarak, R. (2004). Iraq War Ushers in Web-Based Era. In R. Berenger, Global Media Go to War: Role of News and Entertainment Media During the 2003 Iraq War. Spokane: Marquette Books.

Henry, Clement M. and Springborg, Robert(2001): Globalization and the Politics of Development in the Middle East: (Cambridge, UK):Cambridge University Press.

Herman, E. S. & McChesney, R. W. (1997). The Global Media: The new missionaries of global capitalism. Washington: Cassell.

Howe, Reuel L. (1975). The miracle of dialogue. Minneapolis, MN: Winston Press. http://www.Al-bab.com/

Hudson, M. (2006). Washington and AlJazeera: Face to face: Competitive structures to create Middle East realities, in Emirates Center for Strategic Studies and Research (ECSSR), Arab media in the information age conference proceedings. Abu Dhabi: ECSSR.

Ilmarinen, Jussi(2005): Convergence soon brings added value for end users in the Middle East by AME Info FZ LLC in www.ameinfo.com http://www.ameinfo.com/cgibin/cms/page.cgi?page=print;link=69583.

Ingvoldstad, B. (2007). Lithuanian contests and European dreams. In I. Raykoff & R. Deam (Eds.), A song for Europe: popular music and politics in the Eurovision Song Contest. Burlington: Ashgate.

Internet World Stats. (2008). Internet usage in the Middle East: Middle East internet usage & population statistics. At : http://www.internetworldstats.com/.

Iosifidis, P.,Steemers, J., & Wheeler, M. (2005). European Television Industries. London: British Film Institute.

Istance, D. (2008). Lifelong learning and citizenship: International perspectives,' in Williams, E.and Humphreys, G. (eds.) *Citizenship education and lifelong learning: Power and place*. New York: Nova Press.

Ito, J. (2003). Emergent Democracy. Retrieved June 12, 2008, from http://joi.ito.com/joiwiki/EmergentDemocracyPaper.

Jaafar, A. (2005). 'Star' lights up auds in Iraq: Talent show offers viewers an escape. Variety Aug. 29- Sept.

Jacobson, S. (2009, October 30). *Paranormal activity is most profitable film ever*. The First Post, Retrieved from http://www.thefirstpost.co.uk/55417,news-comment,entertainment,paranormal-activity-is-the-most-profitable-film-ever.

Jenkins, Henry(2001), Digital Renaissance. Technology review http://web.mit.edu/cms/People/henry3/converge.pdf.

Jones, Steve,. (1994). "Unlicensed Broadcasting: Content and Conformity," *Journalism Quarterly*, Vol. 71, No. 2, Summer, 1994.

Kaal, E. (2004). Baltic media advertising market 2003. Retrieved August 3, 2004 from http://www.emor.ee/emg/arhiiv.html?id=1189.

Kamalipour Yahya R. (2005) The Battle of the Airwaves: The Rise and Proliferation of Iranian Satellite TV Channels Also check⊗TBS, 15) in http://www.tbsjournal.com/Kamalipour.html

Kelleher, Tom. 2007. Public Relations Online: Lasting Concepts for Challenging Media. Thousand Oaks, CA: Sage.

Killebrew, K. (November, 2002). Distributive and content model issue Convergence: Defining aspects of mew media in journalisms venture. Paper presented at the Dynamics of Convergent Media Conference.

Kummer, M. (2007). The debate on Internet governance: From Geneva to Tunis and Beyond. Information Polity 12.

Levinson, C. (2005). Egypt's growing blogger community pushes limit of dissent. *The Christian Science Monitor*, August 24, p. 6.

: (2005, August 29). The Christian Science Monitor: Egypt's Online Voices of Dissent. Retrieved April 20, 2008, from AlterNet: http://www.alternet.org/story/24525/

Liedtke, M. (2009, September 25). *Something to tweet about: twitter valued at $1b. PhysOrg,* Retrieved from http://www.physorg.com/news173108253.html Merriam-Webster Online Dictionary. 2009.

Lieven, A. (1994). The Baltic revolution: Estonia, Latvia, Lithuania and the path to independence (2nd ed.). New Haven: Yale University Press.

Lips, M., & Jaap, B. (2005). Who Regulates and Manages the Internet Infrastructure? Democratic and Legal Risks in Shadow Global Governance. Information Polity 10.

Longworth, N. (2002). *Making lifelong learning work: Learning cities for a learning century.* New York: Routledge.

Lubbers, Ruud& Koorevaar, Jolanda. (2000) "*Primary Globalisation, Secondary Globalisation, and the Sustainable Development Paradigm - Opposing Forces in the 21st Century*" in *The Creative Society of the 21st Century: FutureStudies,*France:OECDpp.7-24.Alsoin:http://wiki.media-culture.org.au/index.php/Global_Communication.

Lynch, M. (2003). Beyond the Arab street: Iraq and the Arab public sphere, *Politics & Society,* 31(1) pp. 55-91.

:(2004). Shattering the politics of silence: Satellite television talk shows and the transformation of Arab political culture,' *Arab Reform Bulletin,* December 2004, Volume 2, Issue 11, at: http://www.carnegieendowment.org/publications/index.cfm?fa=view&id= 16242.

:(2006). *Voices of the new Arab public: Iraq, al-Jazeera, and Middle East politics today.* New York: Columbia University Press.

:(2007). Blogging the New Arab Republic. Retrieved June 12, 2008, from *Arab Media& Society:* http://www.arabmediasociet y.com/topics/index.php?t_article=32

Magazine Online. Retrieved March 24, 2008 from *http://www.magazine.ucla.edu/features/daily-bruin-newspaper/index.html.*

Malone, Michael "Study: Local TV Easily People's Main Source for New."
Broadcasting and Cable.
http://www.broadcastingcable.com/index.asp?layout=articleID=CA65365
96 Date posted February 28, 2008. Date accessed March 1, 2008.

Mansell, R. and Wehn, U. (1998). *Knowledge societies: Information technology for sustainable development.* New York, United Nations Commission on Science and Technology for Development/Oxford University Press.

Mansour, M. (2007, November 3). Is blogging a bursting bubble? Retrieved June 12, 2008, from Daily News Egypt:
http://www.dailystaregypt.com/article.aspx?ArticleID=10091

Masloski, A. (2008, May 8). Fiction meets reality in Egypt. Retrieved June 14, 2008, from Middle East Times:
http://www.metimes.com/Opinion/2008/05/08/fiction_meets_reality_in_e gypt/2658/

McChesney, Robert M., "The FCC's Big Grab: Making Media Monopoly Part of the Constitution," *Counterpunch*, May 16, 2003, no pagination.

McIntosh, C. (2005). Introduction, in McIntosh, C. and Z. Varoglu. *Perspectives on distance education: Lifelong learning and distance higher education.* Paris: UNESCO Publishing.

McPhail, L. Thomas(2006). *Global Communication: Theories, Stakeholders, and Trends.*(2nd ed).Malden, MA. Blackwell Publishing.

Media Sustainability Index (MSI) – Middle East & North Africa (MENA). (2005). Retrieved June 15, 2008, from IREX:
http://www.irex.org/programs/MSI_MENA/2005/MSIMENA05_summary .asp

Media.ME.com. (2008). GCC media corners $3.7bn of advertising spend, against $733m for the entire Levant region. At:
http://mediame.com/taxonomy/tags/pan_arab_research_center.

Merriam-Webster Online. 18 February 2009. http://www.merriam webster.com/dictionary/blog

Meyrowitz, Joshua. 1985. No Sense of Place. New York: Oxford University Press.

Miles, H. (2003). *Al Jazeera: The inside story of the Arab news channel that is challenging the West*. London: Grove Press.

Miller, William C. 1986. The Creative Edge: Fostering Innovation Where You Work. Reading, MA: Addison-Wesley. "Risk & Reward," Broadcasting & Cable. March 17, 2008.

Misiunas, R. & Taagepera, R. (1993). The Baltic states: Years of dependence 1940-1990 (expanded and updated ed.). Berkeley: University of California Press.

Moreno, J. (2005). *Learning to teach in the knowledge society: Final report*, World Bank, Washington, D. C.

National Broadcasting Company v. U.S., 319 U.S. 190 (1943).

Neher, W. William.(2003)(Development Communication in Africa, Concepts and Case Studies in Kwadwo Anokwa, el, International Communication: Thomson Wadsworth: United States 2003.

Nguyen, P. (October 2, 2007). i-Comm Student Media: New student media organization, i- Comm, aims to give communication students up-to-date real-world experience. *Scroll Online*. Retrieved March 24, 2008from http://www.byui.edu/scroll/campus/2007/10/20071002-i-comm-student media. htm.

Ostrow, A. (2009, April 6). *Twitter and Myspace post huge growth numbers in March*. Retrieved from http://mashable.com/2009/04/06/twitter-and-facebook-post-huge-growth-numbers-in-march/.

: (2009, March 16). *Twitter now growing at staggering 1,382 percent.* Mashable, Retrieved from http://mashable.com/2009/03/16/twitter-growth-rate-versus-facebook/.

Palmer, Allen(2007), Following the Historical Paths of Global Communication, in Yahya R. Kamalipour, Global Communication(2007), 2nd ed.,: Australia and United States: Thomson, Wadsworth.

Pesce, A. (January 23, 2008). Convergence makes headlines for collegiate publications. *The Daily Bruin*. Retrieved March 24, 2008 from http://www.dailybruin.ucla.edu/news/ 2008/jan/23/convergence-makes-headlines-collegiate-publication/.

Petrie, S. and Farima, A. (February 21, 2008). Panelists give insight into online journalism.*Tennessee Journalist*. Retrieved March 24, 2008 from http://tnjn.com/2008/feb/21/ panelists-give-insight-into-on/.

Pew Center for Civic Journalism .(2008). At: http://www.pewcenter.org/doingcj/.

Phipps, Steven.(1991). "The Commercial Development of Short Wave Radio in the United States, 1920-1926," *Historical Journal of Film, Radio, and Television*, Vol. 11, No. 3, 1991.

:2001)"'Order Out of Chaos:' A Reexamination of the Historical Basis for the Scarcity of Channels Concept," *Journal of Broadcasting & Electronic Media*, Vol. 45, No. 1, 2001.

:(1991). "Unlicensed Broadcasting and the Federal Radio Commission: The 1930 George W. Fellowes Challenge," *Journalism Quarterly*, Vol. 68, No. 4, 1991.

: (1990)."Unlicensed Broadcasting in the U.S.: The Official Policy of the FCC," *Journal of Broadcasting & Electronic Media*, Vol. 34, No. 2, 1990.

Pollock, D. (1992). *The Arab street: Public opinion in the Arab world*. Washington, D. C.: The Washington Institute.

Ranney, Austin. (1983). *Channels Of power*. New York: Basic Books.

Reporters Without Borders. (2006, June 22). Retrieved June 14, 2008, from *Police Free Award-* Winning Blogger Alaa Abd Al Fattah: http://www.rsf.org/article.php3?id_article=17660

: (2006, November 7). Retrieved June 24, 2008, from *List of the 13 Internet enemies*: http://www.rsf.org/article.php3?id_article=19603

Rheingold, H. (1992/2000). *Virtual Communities: Homesteading on the electronic frontier*. Cambridge: MA: MIT Press.

Rhinesmith, Stephen(1996) *A Manager's Guide to Globalization: Six Skills for Success in a Changing World*. Chicago: Irwin Professional Publishing.

Rochlin, G. I. (1997). Trapped in the Net: The Unintended consequences of Computerization. Princeton, NJ: Princeton University Press.

Rogers, E. (2003). *Diffusion of innovations*. New York, NY: Free Press.

Saja, K., Rybelis, A., Mickevičius, D., Šimkūnas, Ladukas, Č., & Zibucas, I. (1992). Lithuania 1991.01.13: *Documents testimonies comments*. Vilnius: State Publishing Center.

Sakr, N. (2007). *Arab television today*. London: Tauris Publishers.

: (2001). Satellite Realms: Transnational Television, Globalization and the Middle East. London: *I.B.* Taurus.

Salamandra ,Christa.(2003). London's Arab Media and the Construction of Arabness. http://www.tbsjournal.com/Archives/Spring03/salamandra.html

Salsberg, B. (2003, September). Some advice for Journalism Students. *Communicator,* 10-12.

Schaffer, J. (2004). 'The Role of newspapers in building citizenship,' keynote speech at 5th Brazilian Newspaper Congress, São Paulo, Brazil, September 13, 2004.

Schiller, H. (1996). Information inequality . New York: Routeledge.

Schleusener, L. (2007, February). From Blog to street: The Bahraini public sphere in transition . Retrieved June 14, 2008, from Arab Media & Society: http://www.arabmediasociety.com/countries/index.php?c_article=34

Shannon, V. (2008, March 6). Social Networking Moves to the Cellphone. The *New York Times*.

Shapiro, Stephen J.,(1999). "One and the Same: How Internet Non-Regulation Undermines the Rationales Used to Support Broadcast Regulation," *Media Law & Policy*, Vol. 8, Fall 1999.

Simile; Aug 2005, Vol. 5 Issue 3. "The Arab Information Project Specialists Workshops: Jon Anderson of Catholic University speaking on the expansion of the Internet in the Middle East and Evelyn Early, an anthropologist with the US Information Agency, talking about the role of radio and television in Arab society.
http://www.georgetown.edu/research/arabtech/workshop.htm.

Soriano, Josephine,(2006)."Note: The Digital Transition and the First Amendment: Is it Time to Reevaluate Red Lion's Scarcity Rationale?" *Boston University Public Interest Law Journal*, Vol. 15, Spring 2006.

Sparks, C. (2005). Media and Global Public Sphere: An Evaluative Approach. In W. D. Yong, M. Shaw, & S. Neil, Global Activism Global Media (pp. 34-49). London. Ann Arbor: Pluto Press.

Sun, S. L., & Barnett, G. A. (1999). The International Telephone Network and Democratization. *Journal of the American Society for Information Science.*

Szegedy-Maszak, Marianne. "Mysteries of the Mind: Your Unconscious is Making Your Everyday Decisions," *US News & World Report* pp. 52-58. Feb. 28, 2005.

Tahawy, M. A. (2006, November 16). *Blogs and women force sexual harassment onto Egypt's agenda.* Retrieved March 4, 2008, from http://www.saudidebate.com/index.php?option=com_content&task=view &id=432&Itemid=166

Tanner, A., & Duhe, S. (2005). Trends in mass education in the age of media Convergence: Preparing students for careers in converging news environment. *Studies in Media and Information Literacy Education*, 5, 3, 1-13.

:Trends in Mass Media Education in the Age of Media Convergence: Preparing students for careers in a converging news environment.

Tarawnah, N. (2008). Presentation "Case Study: The Black Iris Blog". United Nations University- International Leadership Institute. Amman Jordan March 15.

The Report, *Kuwait*. (2009). Oxford Business Group.

The Report, *Qatar*, (2009). Oxford Business Group.

Thierer, Adam, (2007) "Why Regulate Broadcasting? Toward a Consistent First Amendment Standard for the Information Age," *Journal of Communications Law & Policy*, Vol. 15, 2007.

Time Warner Entertainment Co.(1997). v. Federal Communications Commission, On Suggestions for Rehearing *In Banc*, U.S. Court of Appeals for the District of Columbia Circuit, February 7, 1997, Document No. 93-5349.

Toffler, A. (1980). *The Third Wave*. New York: Morrow.

Tompkins, A. I (2001). *Convergence needs a leg to stand on*. Retrieved July 26, 2005, ...www.informaworld.com/index/787948466.pdf

Trauth, Denise M., and John L. Huffman, "The Pacifica Case: The Supreme Court's New Regulatory Rationale for Broadcasting," ERIC Document No. ED 184 149, 1979.

UAE most wired country in Arab world. (2008, June 2). Retrieved June 10, 2008, From   *Gulfnews.com*: http://archive.gulfnews.com/technology/developments/10218075.html

UNDP. (2003). *Arab human development report: Building a knowledge society*. New York: UNDP Publishing.

UNESCO. (2004). *Learning: The treasure within*. Paris: UNESCO Publishing.

: (2005). *Towards knowledge societies*. Paris: UNESCO Publishing.

Van Grove, J. (2009, August 24). *Twitter* effect redux: 78% of tweets about Inglorious Basterds were positive. *Mashable Social Media Guide*, Retrieved from http://mashable.com/2009/08/24/inglourious-basterds-tweets/. (http://www.merriam-webster.com/dictionary/blog)

Vernon, Tom."With Radio Blogs, Stations Practice the Art of the Possible," *Radio World*. pp. 1, 6, 8. Feb. 1, 2008.

Wallace, Ruth A. & Alison Wolf. 1986. (1980). *Contemporary Sociological Theory: Continuing the Classical Tradition* 2nd ed. Englewood Cliffs, NJ: Prentice-Hall.

Wallace, Jonathan D., (1999). "*Supreme Court's Rulings Threaten Free Speech*," *USA Today*, March 1999 (exact date and page number unknown).

Ward, W. (2007, February). Uneasy Bedfellows: Bloggers and mainstream media report the Lebanon conflict. Retrieved June 14, 2008, from *Arab Media & Society:* http://www.arabmediasociety.com/topics/index.php?t_article=52

Weblogs soar in Gulf states . (2006, June 26). Retrieved June 14, 2008, from *Al Jazeera English Website*: http://english.aljazeera.net/English/archive/archive?ArchiveId=23619

Whitaker, Brian. http://www.*al-bab.com*/arab/about.htm.

Williams, C. (2008, February 25). *Morocco jails Facebook faker*. Retrieved June 14, 2008, from The Register: http://www.theregister.co.uk/2008/02/25/morocco_prince_facebook_sentence/

Williams, R. (2003).Television: *Technology and cultural form* (Rutledge Classics edition). New York: Rutledge Classics.

World Electronic Media Forum: *World Summit on the Information Society Broadcasters' Declaration;* Tunis 15-17 November 2005. http://aipnew.wordpress.com

www.http://www.nytimes.com/2009/06/16/ 16media.html

Yankelovich, D. (1991). *Coming to public judgment*. Syracuse, NY: Syracuse University Press.

Zayani, M. (2005). *The Al Jazeerah phenomenon*. Boulder, CO: Paradigm Publishers.

Zekri, M. (2008). *Steps on the Road. Mutual Support Between the Internet and Human Rights*. Cairo: The Arab Network For Human Rights Information

Zuckerman, E. (2006, September 16). Alaa on Egyptian Blogs and Activism. Retrieved June 12, 2008, from *My heart's in Accra*: http://www.ethanzuckerman.com/blog/2006/09/16/alaa-onegyptian- blogs-and-activism/

INDEX

Jabbar A. Al-Obaidi

Dr. Jabbar A. Al-Obaidi received his Ph.D. in Communication and Media from the University of Michigan, Ann Arbor, an MA from Hartford University, Connecticut, and a BA from Baghdad University. He is currently Professor and Chairperson of Communication Studies Department and the Director of the Middle East Studies Program at Bridgewater State University, Massachusetts. Dr. Al-Obaidi writes extensively about media in the Middle East and Islamic countries. He also produces television programs and documentary films.

William G. Covington, Jr.

Dr. William G. Covington, Jr. has a Ph.D. from Bowling Green State University. He is on the faculty of Edinboro University of Pennsylvania and he has taught at colleges and universities in Missouri, Ohio, Indiana, and Massachusetts. Additionally, Dr. Covington has held seminars for media organizations in Europe, the Middle East, and Asia. He has published widely on media regional and global management issues in the era of media convergence.